ESSENTIALS OF LEADERSHIP

THE POWER AND KNOWLEDGE TO LEAD AND
MANAGE IN A POSITION OF STRENGTH

ALEX BERMUDEZ

© **Copyright 2022 - All rights reserved.**

The content contained within this book may not be reproduced, duplicated or transmitted without direct written permission from the author or the publisher.

Under no circumstances will any blame or legal responsibility be held against the publisher, or author, for any damages, reparation, or monetary loss due to the information contained within this book, either directly or indirectly.

Legal Notice:

This book is copyright protected. It is only for personal use. You cannot amend, distribute, sell, use, quote or paraphrase any part, or the content within this book, without the consent of the author or publisher.

Disclaimer Notice:

Please note the information contained within this document is for educational and entertainment purposes only. All effort has been executed to present accurate, up to date, reliable, complete information. No warranties of any kind are declared or implied. Readers acknowledge that the author is not engaged in the rendering of legal, financial, medical or professional advice. The content within this book has been derived from various sources. Please consult a licensed professional before attempting any techniques outlined in this book.

By reading this document, the reader agrees that under no circumstances is the author responsible for any losses, direct or indirect, that are incurred as a result of the use of the information contained within this document, including, but not limited to, errors, omissions, or inaccuracies.

CONTENTS

Introduction 5

1. ESSENTIAL PEOPLE SKILLS TO MASTER 11
2. THE LEADER WITHIN YOU 35
   Discovering the Leader in You 39
   A Leader's Purpose 41
   Surrounding Yourself With Diversity 49
   Leading by Example 52
   Leaders Need Coaching and Direction Too 55
3. A LEADER'S STATE OF MIND 63
   Accepting Failure With a Leadership Mindset 71
   Identifying as a Leader 75
   Transitioning Into Leadership 81
   Developing a Leadership Mindset in Current Times 87
4. LEADER RESPONSIBILITY 93
   Ownership: The Key to Becoming an Exceptional Leader 96
   Leadership Lessons From History 103
5. LEADER ACCOUNTABILITY 111
   Demonstrating Accountability 117
6. MASTERY OF SELF—THE DISCIPLINED LEADER 129
   Developing Self-Discipline 132
   A Disciplined Leader in the Digital Age 137

7. MANAGING AND LEADING
   SUCCESSFULLY   145
   Managing Effectively   150
   Leading Effectively   156
   Taking a Closer Look at Ethics   160

   Conclusion   173
   Bibliography   179

INTRODUCTION

It's the small things that make the biggest difference. In my 22 years of leadership, I've come to embrace simple, memorable leadership acts and practices—small changes in behavior such as actively listening, asking questions, and becoming mindful of the example I set. One of my staple practices has been a weekly high-bandwidth one-on-one. I used it to build trust with team members. Apart from building trust, the meeting symbolized my commitment as a leader. It was the first meeting I'd add to my calendar, and it was the last meeting I'd ever consider moving or canceling. It has been a leadership success secret of mine for years. I've learned early on that leadership rests on three truths:

- Mastering that aspect of a person's intellect to lead and manage confidently is vital to success in our modern world.
- Developing the leader in you and having the mindset of one can unlock overlooked possibilities.
- Taking responsibility and being accountable as you master yourself to be a disciplined and successful leader creates strong teams and balanced leaders.

When our leadership is based on these truths, common leadership problems can turn into growth opportunities. These problems can range from difficulties communicating effectively or clearly with peers, managing conflict, dealing with confrontational situations, confronting performance meeting expectations, and other situations teachers, coaches, supervisors, managers, and other leaders routinely find themselves in. When leadership is firmly rooted in these truths, leaders benefit from better-developed communication skills and improved conflict resolution and mediation skills.

These weekly meetings did more than improve team performance; it gave me a front-row seat to an interesting observation. Meetings that focused on real bidirectional conversations about important topics always produced the best outcomes. That's because in these meetings, I've learned to productively fill time. These meetings were an opportunity to renew trust within my team and build on a foundation of respect. It was a safe environment for team members to share ideas, but it was also an accountable environment. I also made it a habit to communicate my expectations at the start and end of the meeting. Even though the meetings were only 30 minutes, it's always a good idea to give people a brief reminder of the important points. A lot can be said in half an hour, so I made a point of it to spotlight the important stuff near the end of meetings. These simple meetings formed the glue that kept multidisciplinary teams together, but the power of these meetings is best witnessed firsthand.

You might think that meetings sound like a lot of work, but so is responsible leadership. I'll share a small spoiler with you: Leadership can't be hacked, no matter what the latest social media trend claims. There is no shortcut or quick way to become a leader that others want to follow. Leadership is a skill that needs to be nurtured. It requires patience, practice, and thoughtfulness. Learning materials are helpful guides, but ultimately, leadership skills need to be developed as we grow and learn in our occupations. It starts with a willingness to embrace change and the courage to take a sober look at oneself. Yes, the leadership road is a tough one, but it is filled with countless opportunities for personal and professional growth.

A Note About the Book

This is not an ordinary book. There are two ways you can go about reading this book: normally or randomly. Allow me to clarify. Many of the chapters in this book are stand-alone topics related to the theme of leadership. Each of these chapters focuses on one important aspect of leadership, e.g., accountability, communication skills, authenticity, leadership mindset, and discipline. If you feel like you need help on a specific topic, feel free to read the chapter of your choice. The book can also be read from start to finish, which provides a more comprehensive overview.

Reading and applying the underlying principles of this book will give you confidence and the knowledge to manage difficult situations. These same principles helped others and myself to manage and lead successfully. The journey to leadership success was not an easy one, though. I grew up and lived in Hawaii (Maui), then moved to Florida with my family. Humble beginnings did not prevent me from achieving personal independence. As I grew and matured as a leader, I gained insight into how to deal with and manage the daily frustrations leaders face in the workplace. Sharing these insights with countless new and stagnant leaders and managers helped them become proactive, passionate leaders that impact people's lives. They led with confidence, and you can too. Now, only one question remains: Are you ready to discover the leader in you too?

1

ESSENTIAL PEOPLE SKILLS TO MASTER

Nearly half a century ago, the United States military coined a phrase that shaped the way we think about leadership. The phrase in question? Soft skills. The term is a bit of a misnomer as "soft" carries connotations of malleability and fragility with it—qualities that we would not look for in a leader. That's why experts are advocating for the term to be tweaked and called "power skills" instead (Agarwal, 2018). I'll be referring to these skills as people skills or soft skills. Decades of research have shown that the most effective leaders are those who have highly developed people skills, i.e., soft skills.

People skills are those characteristics needed to form connections with others. Forming connections with others is a powerful thing and has the potential to unite a team toward a common goal. We see people skills in action in sports all the time. One of the most poignant examples that come to mind is Jürgen Klopp. Before the German coach with the electric smile was signed, Liverpool FC was suffering through a dry spell. In 2020, this changed when the team finally bagged its first Premier League title in three decades (Brennan, 2022)! Klopp had turned things around for Liverpool, and he did so by being an effective leader. This begs the question, what makes an effective leader? Did Klopp turn things around because he recruited better players and focused on team building? Not quite. Klopp's leadership style reinvigorated Liverpool's soccer culture, and the effect could visibly be seen in the quality of matches and fervent fan support.

The best workforce in the world will not perform amicably under poor leadership. As leaders, it is our responsibility to recognize the potential that lies dormant in our teams and to find ways to bring that potential to the surface. Your people skills and your ability to deal with conflict are the secret sauce to winning cooperation with people inside and outside of your company. It worked for Klopp and many other influential managers of high-stakes teams. The very first step is to lessen the degrees of separation between yourself and your team.

Authenticity

There are two lessons leaders need to learn before they can continue their development. Firstly, your team is human. Secondly, each individual on your team is unique. The obvious should be stated, as many leaders seem to forget this fundamental truth. As humans with unique needs and perspectives, we truly appreciate it when someone takes a genuine interest in our thoughts, interests, and long-term well-being. Once leaders have come to terms with the concept that their workforce consists of human beings with needs outside of work, they can begin to build a bridge that fosters trust and team spirit. Small gestures can turn the work environment from robotic to a nurturing environment that encourages teamwork. Start with the smallest of gestures:

- Remember the names of your personnel.
- People love to talk, so allow them to talk about themselves (Kelfer, 2018).
- Make your workforce feel good with well-deserved compliments.
- Appreciate the effort your team puts in to achieve a goal.
- Small gestures of kindness go a long way to building team spirit and improving employee loyalty. Nobody wants to obey a slave driver.

- Listen when members of your team have something to share.
- Smile! Your face won't fall off, nor will you be seen as weak. On the contrary, a genuine smile can make people feel seen which can do wonders for teamwork.

Being authentic is a two-way street. We have to show genuine interest first for it to be reciprocated. That's part of the process of building connections with people. So ask yourself: Would you want to work for yourself? The answer to this question may very well lie in the quality of interactions you have with your team. Remember, it only takes one person to make others feel like they are valued and respected. Are you that person for your team?

Develop Impeccable Communication Skills

Leaders need to have effective communication skills as their ability to communicate with others can directly impact employee morale, productivity, and team satisfaction. Effective communication gets the message across with fewer misunderstandings, which can lead to improved productivity and team morale—all of these are factors that impact a leader's success. Keep the points below in mind to elevate your communication skills:

- ***Know your audience***: Whether you are composing an email, preparing for a meeting, or collaborating with another team, effective communication starts by considering your audience and adapting the message accordingly. A leader needs to be able to *sell* the concept or project they are working on without getting bogged down by nitty-gritty details. Consider who the message is meant for, and tailor it accordingly. The goal is to communicate with the audience on their level.
- ***Listen***: Good listening skills are a vital part of being an effective communicator. Listening is not simply waiting for the other speaker to finish, so you can have a turn. Truly listening to another human being entails resisting that temptation to shoot back with a reply before the other person is done speaking. People who are habitually cut off while trying to air their thoughts are far less likely to speak up, which can and will have long-term consequences. Instead of cutting the other person off, spend the time actively listening to what the person has to say. Use nonverbal cues (like nodding) to show that you are listening, and ask questions to clarify ambiguous points. Be patient while listening, especially if the person trying to

communicate struggles or is anxious. A little patience goes a long way.

- **Hone your writing skills**: The value of written communication cannot be overstated in the workplace. The professional setting demands of us to write well; this means checking that email for typos and clarity of meaning before hitting the send button. Avoid industry lingo, and strive to relay your message as simply and clearly as possible. Proofread, and use grammar checkers to ensure emails, memos, presentations, reports, and other written content that leave your desk are error-free and easy to understand.
- **Talk like a leader**: Great communicators like Simon Sinek and Steve Jobs have one thing in common: They speak clearly while building rapport with their audience. How do they do this? Simple. You need to answer the one question every audience member has; it does not matter if they are executives, employees, or the president. They all want to know one thing: *Why should I care?* In other words, what is your value proposition to the listeners? The audience will lose interest very quickly if they can't determine what benefit they will gain from

listening to your speech. So take the time to refine your message beforehand.
- **Deliver presentations confidently**: There's a fine line between confidence and arrogance. Arrogance relies on boasting about your skills. Confidence is the positive expression of your abilities. It's akin to helping a friend who's struggling with their homework; you're using your skills to help that person. When it comes to presentations, confidence is key, and you'll need to approach it with the same demeanor as one would when helping a friend with homework. You can't expect to help someone if you don't know what's going on, so you'll need to research, prepare, and practice the presentation beforehand. Anticipate possible questions, and keep the answers ready, and you'll be well on your way to delivering presentations confidently.
- **Get the point across**: Be clear and concise in your communication attempts. Whether you are writing an email or delivering a speech, keep your messaging free from jargon. If you can't explain the essence of your message so that a child can understand it, revise what you are trying to say. When writing emails, start by going over the most critical action items in the

first few lines, and use the rest of the email for context. Don't ramble, and keep your messaging relevant to the topic at hand.
- ***Give the keyboard a break***: Computers play such a prominent role in communication in our personal and professional lives. Whether it is a text message or email, bear in mind that not all topics are suitable to discuss in an electronic medium. For sensitive or complex topics, it's best to pick up the phone or discuss them in person. A quick conversation can get the point across much more effectively than strings of emails, and connecting personally helps to build rapport and establish trust—necessary ingredients to improve your efficiency as a leader.

Compassion and Empathy Makes for Strong Leaders

Silk is a fascinating material. Pound for pound, its strength surpasses that of steel, yet it feels luxurious to the touch, making it a prized commodity. A valued leader has a lot in common with silk: They are strong yet flexible enough to adapt to the situation. Much like the silk used in parachutes, compassionate leadership takes a gentler but firm approach to traditional leadership models. Advocates for a compassionate leadership style like Bill Ford and Jeff Weiner have been touting the merits of a gentler leadership style for years. Weiner made compassionate leadership a core value in his company (Collins, 2014). Despite these high-flying role models, male leaders appear somewhat reluctant to embrace compassionate management, as it is erroneously associated with an effeminate role. It's not surprising that female leaders naturally assume a more compassionate management style; however, this does not mean that compassion and strong leadership are mutually exclusive. It's quite the opposite. Just like silk which is strong yet flexible, compassionate leaders know that their management style has a direct impact on the company's bottom line simply by creating a happier work environment. No employee will deliver their best results if they feel like indentured servants or if their leader emulates the fear-mongering styles of *corporate dinosaurs.*

Effective leaders recognize that their team members expect a degree of understanding and respect. That's where empathy comes in. Empathy is the ability to walk a mile in someone else's shoes, but walking that mile is pointless unless it's followed by positive action. As a leader, you need to understand where your team members are coming from and their emotions, stresses, strengths, and weaknesses so you are better placed to take action when the time arises. In the simplest terms, empathy and compassion underpin the support that you should provide your team, just like the silk in a parachute.

Another reason why compassionate leadership styles create better and healthier work environments is their power in diffusing tension and opposition. It is all too easy to dismiss opposers as deliberately antagonistic individuals, quashing any potential growth that may stem from it. Taking a compassionate approach and truly listening to what the opposition has to say encourages debate and allows leaders to make better-informed decisions. Opposition can take many forms that guide the actions, motivations, and values of the individual. Recognizing the different forms of opposition makes it much easier to handle them with compassion. In any leadership or team scenario, we'd likely find the following:

- *Alarmists*: These individuals are motivated by safety and security, so anything that they perceive as a threat to their safety net will send their warning bells ringing.
- *Traditionalists*: Motivated by maintaining the status quo, these individuals tend to oppose change simply because it speaks to a new and unproven way of doing things.

- **Realists**: They are motivated by what is tangible, practical, and the evidence that lies behind the decisions made.
- **Blockers**: These individuals are motivated by safety, security, and maintaining the status quo, and their actions are geared toward preventing new changes from taking effect.
- *"Yes-men"*: They tend to be motivated by personal advancement and status. They'll readily agree with you, but it does not mean they will deliver on their promises.

Upon closer inspection, you may find that the different types of opposition have a common thread: It is driven by a clash of values or underpinned by a fear of some sort. Confronting these fears and finding common ground is the best way to constructively diffuse tension and requires a degree of emotional intelligence.

Emotional intelligence goes beyond recognizing your own and others' feelings. It is the ability to manage your emotions and those of others as well (Brusman, 2021). Let's say a student approaches a teacher because he worries about his exams. The emotionally intelligent teacher will recognize emotion (worry) within the student and motivate him to take certain steps to reduce the worry constructively. The teacher might suggest that the student join a study group or find a tutor to reduce the worry about pending exams while obtaining good results. An emotionally tone-deaf teacher would outright dismiss the student as lazy or would not take their concerns to heart. The same can be said for leaders in various roles. Emotionally intelligent leaders have a deep understanding of themselves and can manage both themselves and others to achieve a common goal. Once again, silk comes to mind. It is a material that is strong and flexible but still feels good to the touch.

Embrace the Mediator Role When Necessary

There are difficult moments in any team that a leader needs to deal with. Team members may not share the same ideas, opinions, or ideals, and on occasion, this can lead to disagreements. It falls to the leader of the team to put the issue to bed and to ensure that personal opinions don't get in the way of accomplishing the goal. These situations call for the leader to adopt a mediator role to handle disputes. Fortunately, there are several steps leaders can take to ensure a successful outcome.

- *Transparent conversation*: Create an open and honest environment where team members can freely speak about their issues. Transparency is key, and the leader should only step in to mediate if parties can't be respectful or resolve the issue (Forbes Human Resources Council, 2019).

- **Use some tact**: Language should help all parties involved to understand what is happening, but it needs to be used tactfully, especially when playing mediator. Phrases like, "My understanding of what you are saying is…" are useful to use in the mediation situation as it allows the speaker to express themselves professionally and personally. It also opens an avenue for respectful discussion which can lead to a positive resolution of the matter.
- **The five-minute rule**: Allow each team member involved in the dispute to share their thoughts uninterrupted for five minutes. Clearing the air and understanding all sides of the story are vital to putting misunderstandings to bed and can help to forge a stronger team.
- **Remain impartial**: The worst thing leaders can do is to pick sides when disagreements arise. Favoritism corrodes teamwork, even though settling disputes may require leaders to side with one employee or another. The leader should decide what is best for each party involved and clearly explain the reasoning behind the decision.

- ***De-escalate situations***: Simple actions can reduce animosity when disagreements arise. Allowing parties to air their grievances and actively discouraging negative body language (such as the crossing of arms, aggressive gestures, invasion of personal space, and lack of eye contact) goes a long way toward maintaining peace and fostering better teamwork.
- ***Set a standard of respect***: Aretha Franklin spelled it out perfectly: "R-E-S-P-E-C-T, find out what it means to me." Disagreements are healthy, but it is up to the leader to set the parameters of candor and respect. Leaders are tasked with finding the best solution to the situation and do not have the luxury of taking disagreements personally. This way, your team understands that it is fine to disagree, but the focus should remain on solving the problem at hand.
- ***Be positive***: Contrary to what films and series would have us believe, people don't generally wake up with the agenda to make someone's life difficult. Make a point of it to remind your employees or team members that everyone is trying their best and not intending to be purposefully difficult. Assuming a more

positive mindset can help to set the stage for resolution-focused conversations in the future.

- **Keep the conversation focused on solutions**: Conflict in the team is never an ideal situation but can yield favorable outcomes when handled correctly. The secret is to keep the conversation focused on finding solutions to the problem. Don't allow team members or employees to talk negatively about each other, but encourage solution-focused discussion. Both sides need to commit to finding a solution, or else the problems will escalate.
- **Team building**: Seeing to the completion of a project is only one small part of a leader's role. Arguably one of the most important jobs a leader has is team building. This encourages collaboration among individuals and can drive productivity. Often, team building exercises are done in an off-site meeting where the leader encourages the team to speak about their challenges in a supportive environment.
- **Stick to the facts**: Questions are a powerful thing and can help parties involved in a dispute come to their own conclusions. Questioning should always be focused on the facts and not be feelings-based or associated with conflict. "Why can't you two work together?" and questions of

this ilk should be thoroughly avoided as they can stir up tensions further. Try asking, "Have you tried to correct the situation?" instead. The goal of questioning is not to provide the answers for the disputing parties but to encourage them to come up with answers of their own.
- ***Create mutually beneficial scenarios***: Conflict usually arises around three key areas: goals, responsibilities, and roles. Determine if the team holds conflicting views of the achievability of goals, timing, or measures. If so, make the effort to adjust the goals in such a manner that it creates a win-win scenario for all involved. This usually resolves conflict quickly and effectively. The same train of thought can be applied to conflict resolution with responsibilities and roles.

It may be tempting to mediate disputes whenever they arise, but this does not fix underlying issues. As far as possible, leaders should avoid mediating disputes. Instead, they should encourage employees and team members to solve the problem among themselves. The solution might not be a preferred one, but the outcome tends to be more positive and lasting.

Practice Exceptional Patience

Effective leadership requires a good measure of patience, especially during a crisis. Solutions take time to come into effect; therefore, leaders must maintain their composure. This can be difficult, especially when a culture of quick fixes and instant gratification is in effect. This tendency is reinforced by the digital work world that seems to prize speed above all else (Sluss, 2020).

A handful of years ago, I had a manager who desperately lacked patience. Let's call him James. The work environment was fast paced, and he never had time to listen to the team's concerns. James was tunnel-visioned and could only be approached if you had results to show. Consequently, nobody on the team felt like they could approach him or talk to him. "James won't understand" was the consensus around the watercooler.

You see, James tended to vent his frustrations on the team when times were challenging. This meant that the onus of problem-solving rested solely with the individual, not an ideal situation if you are a green recruit or lack the confidence to work independently. Had James only stepped back and listened once in a while to the concerns of the team, we would have regarded him differently.

As it was, James projected an air of austere, results-driven coldness that left him isolated from his team and roiling in frustration. Needless to say, the staff attrition rate was quite high as employees felt he simply did not care. Ultimately, his lack of patience was the biggest obstacle to the advancement of his career. Don't get me wrong, he was a decent guy outside of work. My only wish for James was that he could see the value in acquiring a modicum of patience. Teams left under his supervision did not last long and neither did his career. His story always comes to mind as a cautionary tale when patience and leadership are used in the same sentence. I always ask myself what leaders can do differently to avoid being exiled at their place of work. The answer came in five steps:

Place Yourself in Another's Shoes

It is fairly easy to make snap judgments about how others manage certain situations. As a leader, one needs to be able to remain objective and remove personal opinions from the matter at hand. Keep in mind that people tend to lose their cool when they start to run on empty. A leader needs to be strong to handle the pressure but remain calm enough to resolve the issue without the situation devolving into a shouting match. An efficient leader will help their team members or employees see the bigger picture and help them to connect the dots to find a solution.

Calmly Evaluate Tension Points Without Bias

Patient leaders can evaluate tension points which helps them anticipate the root causes of problems. Remaining unbiased when evaluating tension points can be difficult, especially when team members are not on the same page with you. It is easy to become frustrated with an employee who does not share your vision for a particular project or client. Instead of dismissing the employee as *difficult*, view the situation as an opportunity that may give you insight into the intentions and thought processes of said employee. It may not be a pleasant encounter, and you may feel like your patience is being tested, but it will afford you the unique opportunity to appreciate and observe the employee's skills up close. Who knows, that employee might be the perfect fit for a future project. You'll never know when you'll discover a diamond in the rough, so be mindful of other people.

Nurture Positivity

A positive attitude makes all the difference. Imagine this scenario: You are stuck in a traffic jam. On your arrival at the office, you are greeted by valued clients from out of town. In this situation, you have a quick decision to make. You could allow the frustration of battling through traffic to show and be a victim of circumstances, or you could rise to the occasion and thank the clients for their visit.

Find Perspective

Solutions to situations can be hard to find, especially when your patience is wearing thin. In these situations, don't force authority on others or try to push a problem away; the problem will only return later. Prudent leaders learn how to pick their battles, but most importantly, they seek counsel when needed. Whenever a situation is testing your patience, it is best to ask a mentor for advice. Sometimes a fresh perspective is all that is needed to solve a problem.

Don't Run Away From Responsibility

When team members or employees don't listen or continuously make excuses, it can be incredibly easy to grow impatient. Approach these situations with the intention to understand why they arose in the first place. The troublesome situation could have originated from several factors, so be prepared that you could be at fault. In these situations, face the music and be accountable. Calmly come to a decision and inform the rest of the team. In this way, you'll earn and retain their respect. The next time your patience is tested, use it as an opportunity for growth. Evaluate your efficacy, maturity, vulnerability, and purpose as a leader. As time passes, you'll discover that the practice of patience leads to the creation of resourceful and composed leaders (Llopis, 2013).

Nurture Tolerance

Zero tolerance is cause for worry. Tolerance is often defined as having a fair and objective attitude toward those who differ from us. This makes it an underpinning value of a functioning society and forms the basis for the First Amendment protections that we enjoy. For this reason, *zero tolerance* attitudes in the workplace can become detrimental.

Every time we tell ourselves, "I can live with X, Y, or Z," we are practicing tolerance, and this does mean we've accepted or understood the situation. Acceptance can only happen when we tolerate something. Think of the times when you showed up late to a meeting. Your late appearance was tolerated but not necessarily accepted. When we accept something, we implicitly tell ourselves that "X, Y, or Z is fine" or at the very least passable (Fish, 2014). Being tolerant is not an easy feat, but there are some steps you can take toward it.

- ***Own your feelings***: Humans are emotional beings, but it is important to recognize that people can only make you feel a certain way if you allow them to. Change your thinking to move from an attitude of blame. Instead of saying to yourself, "Miss X upset me," reframe the situation. "I'm angry because Miss X said or did A, B, and C, but I don't have to stay upset," is a much healthier approach than playing the blame game.

- *Be curious*: Many times, a lack of tolerance stems from a lack of understanding. By embracing an open mindset and learning about the people around us, we can understand and accept others better (Eugene Therapy, 2020).
- *Refresh your perspective*: When we can't see where the other person is coming from, it is incredibly difficult to be tolerant. Shifting your perspective from yourself to appreciating another person's experiences and how they relate to people around them can make a big difference.
- *Respect the individual's autonomy*: We would never want our tightness to think and choose for ourselves being taken away from us; therefore, as leaders, it is our responsibility to extend that same courtesy to others even when we don't agree with them.

Leaders who actively work to develop tolerance in their lives might discover a pleasant side effect: that they are happier and have a greater appreciation of diversity. The majority of work environments will require interaction with people. Now that you know which essential people skills to master, it is time to discover the leader within you.

2

THE LEADER WITHIN YOU

Great leaders are not born. They are groomed. Past research suggests that leadership has remarkably little to do with genetics. Studies lean in favor that leadership is a learned skill and genetics only give us 30% of the picture (University of Illinois College of Agricultural, Consumer and Environmental Sciences [ACES], 2014). The research findings are good news as it implies that anyone can develop the necessary leadership skills with the right guidance.

Leadership skills are in high demand in our fast-paced digital-first world. These skills can be used in any industry and role. Developing the right leadership skills can make the difference between career advancement and being stuck without prospects. Leadership skills cover a wide range of skills, attributes, and personality traits (Indeed Editorial Team, 2021a). Good leaders will have a healthy mix of skills that will serve them well in a variety of roles. The most crucial skills effective leaders strive to develop include the following:

- ***Goal setting***: These skills revolve around the ability to establish objectives by keeping the big picture in mind. Goal setting is done for the common good of the company, project, or team at large and can consist of a series of smaller and larger goals and steps that are necessary to achieve these objectives. Goal setting should make use of the resources available within your team and must be realistic to be achievable.
- ***Communication and delegation***: Effective communication skills not only help our contemporaries to understand us better but also help leaders to determine the best form of communication for specific messages. Some topics are better discussed in person, while others can easily be covered in an email. An effective communicator knows which mode of communication will help to drive the point of their message home. Equally important is the ability to delegate. No leader is expected to do everything alone, so honing your delegation skills can help to free up precious hours in a

busy schedule. When delegating, ensure that the instructions provided are clear and task-specific, and select the team member or employee that is best suited for the task.
- *Dependability and integrity*: Dependability refers to the level of trust we have in someone to complete a task correctly and timely. This quality can be fostered by setting a standard of work ethic that focuses on punctuality, kindness, and being an example for your team. Leading by example also means leading with integrity. Leaders need to be accountable for their actions and mistakes and encourage a culture of honesty.
- *Decisiveness*: The ability to make educated decisions quickly, even under pressure, is a precious one. Effective leaders understand that certain decisions cannot be placed on the back burner and that some situations demand quick action. This does not mean these leaders disregard the potential consequences of their choices. Instead, they aim to minimize potentially negative results by relying on their industry knowledge and experience to make quality decisions quickly. This skill develops naturally as you gain more experience in your industry of choice.

- ***Motivation and conflict management***: The ability to motivate others is a necessary one, especially when team members need to rally to complete tasks and reach goals. Of equal importance is self-motivation. You can't expect your team to be motivated and hardworking if the leader at the helm is a master procrastinator! The key to maintaining motivation in others is conflict management. This skill helps leaders to be successful mediators when the occasion arises —the need for conflict management can arise surprisingly often, especially when people's stances differ on a situation or topic. The skill is crucial to reaching a reasonable compromise for all parties involved.
- ***Team building***: Spotting the strengths and weaknesses in our teams is crucial to reaching goals and objectives. Teamwork becomes essential to achieving those goals. Leaders make use of team building to promote collaboration in their teams. These training and bonding activities help our colleagues get to know each other better, setting the standard of respect.

DISCOVERING THE LEADER IN YOU

Leadership is a gift that keeps on giving. Many who embark on a leadership journey discover that personal development and career progression benefit as well. Leadership is a skill that requires two things: practice and a personal touch. Not everyone leads their teams the same way, so hone your leadership skills by focusing on the following:

- ***Spotting your leadership style***: Personality and management skills add to the diversity of leadership styles that we encounter in the *wild*. The roles we occupy and the industries we work in influence leadership style as well. Leadership is a beautifully unique thing that has no right or wrong way about it. Some may find they lead best by motivating their colleagues, while others naturally gravitate to the front desk. Others are better suited to manage larger goals. Leadership style is as unique as the individual but can only improve with practice. Find opportunities to practice your brand of leadership, whether it be leading by example or motivating people, to refine the skills needed.
- ***Learn from role models***: Looking to proven leaders can help us determine the

characteristics of a specific leadership style one could use in the workplace. Pay attention to how proven leaders used their skills and qualities to complement their leadership styles successfully. The good news is that role models are fairly easy to find. Whether it be a celebrity figure, a stockbroker on Wall Street, or an inspirational employee, role models whom we can learn from are all around us if we are observant.

- *Guidance from mentors*: Learning directly from a leadership figure is a distinct advantage that comes with mentors. Mentors are useful when we want to hone our leadership skills. The mentor could be an industry leader, an experienced colleague, or another person you've identified as a leader. Mentors provide us with feedback on the issues we face, helping to refine our skills healthily and constructively.
- *Discovering leadership resources*: Leadership resources can take many shapes. Keep an eye on articles, publications, or news on the leaders you admire, or try attending talks presented by inspirational figures you admire. There are many resources available, running the full gamut of self-guided options and practical experience. Finding suitable

resources requires a willingness to try new things and learn from the experience of others.

- **Education**: Apart from books, podcasts, and talks, there's a more proactive step we can take in honing our leadership skills—enrolling in a leadership course. There's a wide range of these courses available, and it allows learning from mentors who use proven techniques (Indeed Editorial Team, 2022).

A LEADER'S PURPOSE

What is the purpose of leadership? The answer to this question is no doubt informed by ethics, values, hopes, and unique worldviews. We tend to answer this question based on what matters to us, making it an effective mirror to reflect our internal understanding of why leaders do what they do. Ideally, the purpose of leadership should be evident in our daily actions.

Every successful leader has a purpose tied to their leadership. Don't confuse the purpose of your leadership with the mission statement or some corporate vision. The purpose is a distinctly personal thing and revolves around how you define yourself in your circumstances. Our purposes are the ones that inform our leadership style and make a statement of who we are as human beings. Look back on the times when you found yourself in a leadership position, and ask yourself:

- How did you want to lead the project?
- What feedback do you think your colleagues would have had about your leadership?
- How did you make your colleagues feel?
- What goals have you set yourself?

Your answer to these questions will give you some perspective to work back from. From there, you can start to create and refine your leadership purpose. Be aware that maintaining that purpose is no easy task! You need to be willing to hold yourself accountable for the bigger picture (Dickson, n.d.). Keep in mind that you are only human and that it's completely fine to make mistakes. Effective leadership is a journey of learning after all.

Understanding Purpose-Driven Leadership

Purpose-driven leadership quite literally pays dividends. Research suggests that customers view purpose-driven brands more favorably, generating brand loyalty in the process (Bulgarella, 2018). Yet a gap can exist between what a leader believes their purpose is and their actions.

The purpose is not limited to making a brand unique. In the business setting, it can showcase the organization's evolution. At its most rudimentary, the purpose simply expresses what an organization aspires toward. A company's purpose gives us insight into its evolution. Some companies want to control the status quo, projecting a company culture that's obsessed with results, hierarchy, and power. On the other end of the continuum, we find organizations that have more expansionary views, focusing on innovation. Where an organization would be positioned on this continuum would be reflected in its purpose. A closer analysis of the purpose statement could reveal valuable clues. The purpose should be removed from the organization's current culture; otherwise, it will produce inauthenticity.

Purpose-driven leaders inspire stronger results from their teams. Research revealed even more striking and wide-ranging benefits. Overall, purpose-oriented companies were found to enjoy higher levels of innovation and workforce retention than their rivals. In addition to this, the research found that leaders who had a clear idea of their purpose were twice as likely to find meaning in their work. A lack of understanding of what *purpose* truly means is one of the biggest barriers to this. *Purpose* is a rather nebulous term. One person might describe it in terms of resolve or determination.

Another might point to intentions or objectives as forms of purpose. It could be something else entirely, so having a clearer understanding of purpose helps.

Two Pillars of Purpose

Your vision and the driving force behind your actions, your *why*, are the pillars that support purpose. Your vision should describe what you want to contribute to society in the future. Keep in mind that visions can change over time. Your *why* or driving force is best described as your raison d'être; it never changes and defines who you are. Think of Apple. Their drive is to *think different,* and it defines who they are. Traditional attitudes can be a significant roadblock when trying to understand the purpose. When our focus remains on performance and profit, it becomes easy to miss the bigger picture. This focus on performance brings with it a culture that values male-centric leadership characteristics, such as competitiveness, directness, and dominance.

The idea of making a positive impact in the world is an appealing one. People want to believe that the work they do is meaningful, but it's a subjective experience. My idea of what it means to make a positive impact differs from yours, as yours does from anyone else's. We are individuals, so it is up to us to define our sense of purpose. It may sound like a tall order. Fortunately, there's a simple process that can help.

Three-Step Process

A handy starting point, the three-step process requires us to pay attention to the following:

1. Hone in on Non-negotiables

Understanding what matters to you is crucial when we want to zero in on the non-negotiables in our life. Think of all the things that matter to you, and create a list. Aim to add at least 25 items to the list. These items should focus on the activities you enjoy, the characteristics that define you, your talents and passions, as well as the people you look up to. Once this list is completed, scrutinize it closely, and remove the items that don't truly matter. Combine similar entries, and continue to edit the list until you are left with five words or phrases. These five words or phrases symbolize your *"line in the sand*, the things that are the most important to you.

2. Create a Short Story

After whittling the list down to five words or phrases, it's time to combine them into a brief story that represents what you care about most in life. That's your purpose statement. It's important to be in the right frame of mind when starting this process. Ask yourself:

- What did you love doing as a child? How did that activity make you feel?
- What activities will bring more happiness into your life?
- What are the biggest challenges you faced, and how did they impact you?
- If you could do anything right now, what would you like to do?
- How can your work and personal life contribute toward making your actions matter?

Many of the answers to these questions will likely point to things you haven't considered before or did not fully explore. The results can be pleasantly surprising, especially coming from a results-driven environment that tends to leave us with little bandwidth to consider what gives us purpose.

3. Create Goals to Motivate Action

Purpose without action is about as effective as writing a book but never getting past the planning stage. Uncovering and understanding your sense of purpose is only the start of the journey. The next step is to turn that understanding into something tangible. Take a closer look at the purpose statement that you've crafted. Use the language from your statement to create midterm goals to guide your actions. Normally, the three- to five-year time limit on these goals will give you enough leeway to realistically achieve them. Whether the goal is to secure a promotion or drive innovation, remember to keep the focus on what type of leader you want to be.

Taking responsibility and being accountable as you master yourself to be a disciplined and successful leader is vital to achieving goals. Consider the responsibilities you'll need to take on as you consider your goals. The goal could be a weakness you identified, for example, having difficulties in communicating effectively or clearly with employees and peers. One might decide to improve their soft skills over the next three years to improve communication skills. A leader might choose to actively commit a portion of their time to develop their soft skills and set steps toward achieving these goals. The answer might lie in an educational course, additional training, or elsewhere. The important thing is that we actively work on achieving the goals we decided on. A big part of that is having a long-term vision.

Road mapping key activities and crucial results will have a significant impact on how we achieve our goals. The idea is to keep track of activities and results that will contribute the most toward achieving certain goals. Keep key relationships in mind. While purpose should be deeply personal, leaders still need the support of other people to realize goals.

Those who lead with purpose seem to radiate energy and passion that positively impacts everyone around them. Those leaders seem to have a reputation for attracting talent or aspiring achievement, simply because they have a clear understanding of their *why* and the driving force behind it. There are several characteristics these leaders seem to share, including:

- *A passion for seeing others succeed*: These leaders are vested in achieving their goals successfully and will often place the needs of the team and goals before their own.
- *Approaching work with a sense of urgency*: This makes all the difference, especially during times of change and uncertainty. A healthy sense of urgency is helpful to maintain energy levels and combat work-related fatigue.
- *Actively creating productive atmospheres*: When teams struggle with engagement, productivity, or achieving results, part of the blame falls directly on the leader for not providing clear direction. Leaders need to actively create

productive environments for their teams to function and bloom in.
- *Remaining the same at work and home*: When we observe notable leaders in their personal lives, we often discover the same drive, passion, and discipline which are present as well.
- *Making decisions with a clear purpose in mind*: Activities and initiatives that do not align with the overarching purpose of leadership are not pursued. They are viewed as a distraction.

Leaders with the ability to visualize the outcomes are generally able to set goal-oriented actions in motion to help with goal completion. In this way, they successfully overcome obstacles. Developing leadership with purpose is about creating goals that place one in a position to help others (Gleeson, 2021).

SURROUNDING YOURSELF WITH DIVERSITY

Any high-performing organization or group will be powered by a diversity of thought. Bringing multiple viewpoints to the table has many advantages and brings with it a larger pool of knowledge to inform our decisions. Having people with diverse experiences on your team is especially useful for small businesses. Often these businesses don't have many people to rely on, so a diverse team makes business sense. There are several steps these businesses take to ensure their workforce is diverse in thinking. These steps include the following:

Breaking Down Silos

Leaders who break down silos are rewarded with superior results. By making use of interdisciplinary teams, leaders are trying to encourage diverse thinking. The idea behind this strategy is a simple but proven one: Tackling a challenge from different angles delivers superior results. I'll illustrate this point with an example.

Let's say your company was hired to create a platform for local events. What kind of team do you bring together to make this happen? One company decided a diverse team was the best answer and brought together a team of tech, creative, marketing, and business people to find a solution (Gale, 2019). The solutions they came up with were as diverse as the range of experience that was represented. The tech team suggested that GPS maps should be used, while the creative team drafted original ad campaigns. Each person's input should add value to the project as this will drive innovation.

Evaluating Thinking Styles

Making use of personality assessment lets some leaders take a structured approach. In the corporate world, team members are asked to complete the assessment. The results are shared with the group. The idea is to gently remind everyone in the group that different kinds of thinning add value. The idea is to create an atmosphere where creative ideas trigger the production of more creative ideas. Some leaders take this a step further and look for opportunities to pair dissimilar thinkers on a task. The result? Better collaboration and problem-solving that lead to a high-quality solution.

Using Thinking Techniques

Brainstorming sessions can help to get the creative juices flowing, especially when teams lack diversity of thought. When teams suffer from groupthink and habitually come to similar, unchallenged conclusions, it can be beneficial to direct their collective energies. Instead of asking the team, "What is the best solution to problem X?" asking them to find the next best solution slows things down and forces group members to consider all of their options carefully. Having groups consider the problem from different angles is a good practice. Equally important is encouraging everyone to speak up. The value of accurate assessments and intensive brainstorming is lost if we don't encourage everyone in our teams to speak up. Leaders need to create a space where everyone can feel heard and valued. They must be willing to act as mediators when diverse thinking heats up into conflict.

LEADING BY EXAMPLE

Leading by example is so easy that a child could do it. If you've ever played Simon Says or Follow the Leader, you can lead by example. Leading by example is a style of leadership where we model the behavior we want to encourage in our team members. It goes beyond pushing team members toward excellence and turns the leader into an active role model. Think of it as the difference between telling your team, "You can do this," and showing them how it is done. Leaders who are not afraid to take the helm lay solid foundations of trust and camaraderie in their teams. The result? Better problem-solving and improved foundations of trust and camaraderie in the team. By carrying some of the weight yourself, you are communicating a very important message to your team: You value their work.

Remember when you had to do group projects during school? Every year, the same thing happens: There's one kid in the group who does not contribute. That kid was the biggest reason why I (and many others) dreaded group work. Why should someone share in the benefits if they did not contribute? This is where leading by example makes a significant difference in how teams view their leaders. Engaged leaders demonstrate to their teams that they are invested in their initiatives. Keep in mind that the people you are leading will pay a lot of attention to what you say and do. Inconsistency can lead to frustration and, worse still, a lack of trust. The key is to model the right example to your team. Leading by example has several benefits, including:

- It can inspire people around you, leading to improved motivation in the team.
- It lays a foundation of trust between the leader and team.
- It positively impacts the productivity of team members by creating an inclusive and collaborative work environment.
- It lays the foundation for a culture of accountability.
- It sets an example of excellence for the team.
- It improves employee retention and engagement and is a team-building activity.

The beautiful thing about leadership is that it is unique. Everyone has unique qualities that can make them good leaders. Those who lead by example share an interesting set of qualities. They

- *Get involved*: These hands-on leaders show their teams that they support their work without taking over the initiative. These leaders realize that they have the responsibility of setting the tone for their company culture and prefer to lead from the front.
- *Are People Persons*: Leading is not the same as managing. Good leadership is about motivating and inspiring the team. These leaders have their team's best interests at heart and aren't afraid to give credit where it's due. These leaders will take steps to prevent burnout and create strong teams.
- *Dislike Micromanaging*: A good leader does not micromanage; they are role models. Leading by example does not guarantee your team will do things exactly your way. Micromanaging leads to frustration and hurts motivation. Instead, trust your team to get the work done, and support them where needed.
- *Embrace flexibility*: Flexible leaders can embrace change and find solutions more effectively. This is why flexibility is considered to be a key leadership skill. These leaders accept that plans will change and time lines will shift and adapt as needed.

- ***Truly listen***: Not many people realize this about listening—it's a skill. You'll need to practice the right kind of listening to reap benefits. People listen in two ways: to reply and to understand. When we listen to replies, we have a very limited understanding of what is happening. Listening to reply happens every day, and everybody does it. Your automatic reply when someone greets you with "good morning" is proof. When we listen to understand, comprehending what the other person is saying becomes a priority. Your attention is on understanding context, and you'd likely ask questions, instead of listening to form a reply. This is especially true when we are facing constructive criticism. It can be hard to face feedback that's not flattering, but true leaders use this feedback as a foundation for improvement. They understand that leadership is a learning process.

LEADERS NEED COACHING AND DIRECTION TOO

All leadership skills take time and practice to hone. Leading by example is no exception. Building this skill is worth it, though, as it can help to encourage higher levels of engagement and trust in your teams. As a leadership style that can be widely used, from managing a group of direct reports to leading a team without being a manager, leading by example shows team members that they are valued (Martins, 2021). On the other hand, if the group is led by someone with poor leadership skills, conflict may arise. Think of a CEO who discourages unnecessary spending yet frequently changes the furniture in his or her office. Chances are that the employees won't take this CEO seriously, as he or she is not being an example for the team. If the same CEO discourages unnecessary spending and models the appropriate behavior, employees will likely follow suit. So how does one improve on their leadership skills? Generally, a coach may be the answer.

The role of a leadership coach is to empower the person being coached to surpass their limits, improving skills naturally. Being coached as a leader has some distinct advantages, namely:

- *It enables quality exchanges*: Leaders who make use of a coach have a distinct advantage of benefitting from a mutually beneficial exchange. Both the coach and the person being coached need to use their expertise and experience to critically think about objectives and how they'll be achieved. The approaches used may vary, but the quality of the exchange will be enhanced due to the alignment of common interest: success. Through coaching, leaders become aware of their shortcomings and can discover different ways of achieving their goals.

- **It clarifies goals**: A good coach has the goal of helping the leader (regardless of skill level) obtain all the tools needed to perform their duties. One of these tools is the ability to set clear, purposeful goals that align with the leader's values and company vision. Coaches help leaders to broaden their vision, improve responsibility in their role, and guide them in achieving goals.
- **It refines leadership**: It is no secret that the day-to-day lives of leaders can become occupied with tasks and deadlines. This forces operational priorities to take precedence over long-term vision and strategy. Many business owners find themselves in a similar situation: working in your business as opposed to working on it. When you're drowning in tasks, it becomes incredibly difficult to take a step back and spot where improvement is needed. Failure to delegate tasks successfully often lies at the heart of this situation and is an aspect

that can be improved upon with coaching. Coaches help leaders to reflect on their current situation and delegate where necessary.

- *It values emotional intelligence*: Communication is a crucial part when developing leadership in any context. Many leadership coaches orient their teachings to encourage an awareness of emotional intelligence. When leaders become aware of the important role that emotional intelligence plays, they generally adopt a more benevolent attitude that is centered on communication and a healthy work environment. The emotionally intelligent leader can cultivate enthusiasm and performance in their teams, which is why any leadership coach worth their salt will insist on integrating emotional intelligence practices into the daily routine. Self-awareness and regulation, social awareness, and relationship management are some of the areas a good coach will advise improvement on (Preterit, 2022).

Being coached has many benefits and is a formative experience. Leaders who benefit from coaching can transition out of the coaching phase and embrace the coaching role themselves. A good coach can be viewed as someone who holds up a mirror, forcing you to periodically reexamine yourself and your relationships. It is this introspection that helps us evolve as leaders.

More Than Self-Help

Over the last handful of years, coaching in business has become an increasingly common practice. While coaching within organizations is widely accepted, not many leaders are trained to become coaches themselves. Often, coaching is treated with the airs and graces of top-level executives wanting to *better themselves*. This downplays the impact coaching can have within an organization. The truth is, leadership coaching is far too beneficial to be confined to the upper echelons. In our modern business landscape, there exists a need for leadership coaching to become a component of business philosophy. Instead of reserving leadership coaching as a tool meant for high-level executives, it should form a part of professional development throughout an organization. Understanding the basic assumptions that guide successful coaching can help leaders embrace a coaching role in their organization. These assumptions are as follows:

- ***You already have the answers***: The coach's role is that of a guide. They are not problem solvers, and their purpose is to guide.

- *The coach is only an assistant*: When you receive guidance from a coach, you are accountable for your process. The coach is only an assistant who helps to lay the foundation, but you will need to do the work.
- *The coach is passionate about helping*: These people are driven to see others' success and are passionate about enabling the change process.
- *Coaching is a trust game*: Coaching conversations are confidential, meaning that the client–coach relationship should be treated with the utmost respect.

Keep in mind that connections, not communication, lie at the heart of coaching. Coaching is about connecting on a deeper level, so it makes sense that a good coach should embody certain traits. Look for a coach who

- *Is non-authoritative*: The coaching relationship is one built on cooperation. It is not based on power. The coach is only in charge of the coaching process and the structure thereof; they are not responsible for agenda setting or leading discussions.
- *Is an active listener*: Active listening is a skill that requires us to be mentally present and focused. Coaches who listen actively will ask

clarifying questions and will attempt to understand the core concerns of a matter.
- *Asks powerful questions*: Powerful questions tend to be open-ended in nature. These questions are easy to understand and often start with *how, what, when, where,* or *why*.
- *Doesn't have hidden agendas*: Effective coaches are honest, direct, and respectful. They don't get personally involved and can be counted on to be professional at all times.
- *Provides direction*: The task of a coach is to empower you to reach your goal and produce the desired transformation. Good coaches usually provide you with tasks designed to facilitate that transformation. These tasks could include journaling, writing down certain observations, facing difficult situations, or other tasks that the coach deems necessary. These tasks are intended to refine certain soft skills that are crucial to effective leadership.

Leadership positions come with respect, but it is also a responsibility. As a leader, finding the balance between responsibility and respect is crucial. It is the leader's role to guide and inspire their teams but is also their responsibility to provide guidance and oversight. Coaching within leadership roles can help CEOs, managers, business owners, and teachers motivate their teams effectively while connecting on a deeper level. Proper coaching is one pillar of successful leadership. The other pillar is centered on acquiring the leader's state of mind.

3

A LEADER'S STATE OF MIND

"The pessimist complains about the wind. The optimist expects it to change. The leader adjusts the sails."

— JOHN MAXWELL

Maxwell's words describe the leadership mindset well. Leadership is who you are. It embodies the values and beliefs that are enthroned in our hearts and creates the foundation for how one leads. Understanding and nurturing the leadership mindset is what inevitably separates managers and leaders. Don't be fooled: A manager and a leader are not the same. The roles encourage two very different mindsets. The manager mindset is focused on tasks and typically will not exert effort beyond completing their to-do list for the day. Leaders strive to represent all points of view to ensure a favorable outcome.

Managers are happy to work inside the confines of a plan, while leaders look for ways to improve the plan. The manager mindset tends to be results-oriented and focused on short-term results, while the leader tries to surround themselves with talent. There are many more differences I can point out between managers and leaders, but the key difference that separates managers from leaders lies in their approach to completing tasks. Managers emphasize control to complete tasks, while leaders prefer to influence their team members to deliver their best results. It is all in the mindset.

Mindset is considered to be one of the greatest predictors of success, but nurturing the proper one is no easy feat. Of all the things humans are capable of changing, one's mindset will still prove to be the hardest thing to alter. As a leader, your success depends on what you bring to the table. If you bring valuable contributions to the table, your career evolves. Once again, mindset lies at the heart of the matter.

Shifting to a leader's mindset is a subtle process. It happens in the nuanced shifts that occur in the mind, before delegation or coaching skills are used. You see, the first step we need to take toward nurturing a leadership mindset is to change how we think about ourselves and the roles we occupy. Only after you've evaluated your role as a leader can you select the appropriate mindset to nurture.

- *Growth mindset*: The growth mindset rests on the assumption that people can learn, grow, and expand their stills. When leaders nurture a growth mindset, they become empowered to spot setbacks and opportunities and have the reliance to try again when they encounter failure. Open-mindedness is vital to the development of this mindset, as open leaders are more likely to grow and find development opportunities.
- *Inclusive mindset*: For inclusivity to be truly part of an organization's best practices, it needs to be present in leadership. Inclusivity forms part of the compass that directs the thinking and behavior of leaders. It focuses on gathering perspectives and new ideas. Leaders who practice inclusivity actively seek diversity while being aware of the obstacles that can prevent them from reaching out. Many business owners found that nurturing inclusivity is the shift that

their organization needed to future-proof itself (Meyler, 2018).

- *Agile mindset*: This is best described as having an open and adaptable mindset. An agile mindset is particularly valuable in our rapidly changing work environments. Leaders are expected to absorb, filter, and assess information quickly. This quick speed of information processing helps them to reassess their decisions and anticipate change. Agile leaders are resilient and can spur innovation.
- *Enterprise mindset*: Workplace demands expect modern leaders to increasingly embrace the enterprise mindset. This mindset centers around setting goals for themselves and their teams that will align with the organization's goals. With this mindset, the organization comes first, and decisions are made for the greater good of the organization. These leaders are usually the first to break down siloed thinking for the benefit of the entire organization.

One thing we need to keep in mind about shifting mindsets is that they can only be successful if there is a supportive culture in place. New thinking will not drive leadership success by itself, and the best intentions can fall short if leaders don't model the appropriate behaviors. Every type of mindset has its benefits and drawbacks and should be considered carefully. A company that embraces the growth mindset but punishes failure and risk taking sends a very confusing message. The most likely result is that the employees will not embrace the changes. Similarly, a company that rewards individuals for their efforts will have a hard time instilling an enterprise mindset in its employees.

Mindset drives every action, decision, and opinion in people. It leaks into the culture around us and sets the tone for teams. Mindsets influence every aspect of our lives. Recall the last time you were stuck in traffic. Your mindset will determine whether you fly into a fit of road rage or try to understand why the car in front of you is moving so slowly. Mindset shapes how we focus our effort, but it is not something we are powerless to change. Healthy leadership mindsets can be developed if you are mindful of certain elements.

- ***Willingness to face challenges***: The nature of leadership means that you will be expected to address problems and help your team overcome challenges. A leader will keep their team focused on the outcomes and face any issue head-on. These leaders see problems as opportunities to grow.

- ***Being decisive***: The ability to make decisions quickly, communicate confidently, and stand behind your decisions is a foundational element for strong leadership (Building Champions, n.d.). Impulsiveness undermines leadership, but decisiveness allows leaders to make timely decisions. These leaders understand that moving forward is the most important step and that getting caught in the mire of fears and questions can stall progress.
- ***Embracing humbleness***: Humans are fickle beings. They will not follow a leader who lacks confidence or who appears to be timid and cautious. Nor will they follow a leader who never tasted humble pie. People look for humility in a leader, someone who is not afraid to admit that they don't know something but will take steps to quickly fill in those gaps. A humble leader gives credit where it is due.

When combing through the archives of humble leaders, one name is of particular interest: Nelson Mandela. The Nobel Prize-winning South African experienced it all: from being jailed to liberating South Africa from the clutches of apartheid and becoming president of the nation. Through it all, Mandela remained humble and focused intending to unify the South African people—a goal that was briefly achieved in 1995. In a display of phenomenal leadership, Mandela attended the 1995 Rugby World Cup. South Africa won against their archrival New Zealand. It was a victory for South African rugby and a symbolic triumph for a nation ravaged by segregation. Mandela was highly respected, and in remembrance of his legacy, South Africans dedicate every June 18th as an opportunity to create the change they want to see. None of these positive long-term effects would have happened had Mandela been arrogant or timid.

- *Having strong backbones*: Sometimes, leaders fail to realize that credit for success and failure is distributed differently. You see leaders share in the credit when their teams are successful but accept sole responsibility for failure. These leaders take failures as an opportunity to investigate what went wrong, and their approach needs to be adjusted. They accept the fallout and have to be a guiding star.
- *Having a future-forward mindset*: Successful leaders are comfortable with change. They understand that a fixed mindset is the enemy of innovation. When we nurture fixed mindsets, we risk missing important developments, falling behind, and becoming irrelevant. Failure

to look beyond the here and now results in businesses closing down. Forward-thinking leaders are aware that the world is changing at a fairly fast pace and are not afraid to adapt.

- **Being resourceful**: Strong leaders know the value of a growth mindset. They look to industry leaders for direction and ideas but often cast a wider net. These leaders are not hesitant to work outside of their comfort zone when the right opportunity arises. These leaders are willing to learn from anyone and tend to be open-minded to solutions.
- **Having a heart for people**: A little bit of consideration goes a long way. Leadership comes with a responsibility: to develop people. This stems from a strong desire to see others succeed. Consequently, these leaders strive to provide opportunities for their teams.
- **Embracing honesty and transparency**: Leaders who are transparent and honest have happier team members. That's because transparency builds bonds of trust with team members, who in turn work harder as a result.

ACCEPTING FAILURE WITH A LEADERSHIP MINDSET

Madison Square Garden is synonymous with historical events. One of those events was the championship fight between Muhammad Ali and Joe Frazier. This was 1971, and at the time, Ali was known for his charisma and larger-than-life personality. He was adored, and he was hated. Historians believed that it was Ali's outspoken nature and his political stance that were behind this. Whether it was by design or default, it was Frazier who was positioned as the poster child of patriotism. You see, Ali was banned from boxing for three years after he refused to be drafted for the Vietnam War. This led to him being stripped of the championship title. Ali knew this, but he stuck to his guns and refused to compromise his values. To regain the title, Ali had to beat Frazier.

Up until his match with Frazier, Ali was burning bright on the comeback trail. Confidently, he assured the world that he would dominate Frazier in the ring. The world watched with bated breath as the legend faced his opponent and lost spectacularly. Ali's defeat and how he handled it can be a master class in the art of accepting failure!

Leaders walk a daily tightrope between balancing the needs of customers, stakeholders, the organization, and employees. In an ideal world, these elements would align seamlessly, but reality is a different beast. It is hard, unclear, and messy, so it is not surprising that leaders can fail spectacularly at times. How we deal with failure ultimately separates successful leaders from those who imitate leadership. Here is where we can learn a lot from Ali.

- ***Understand why you failed***: In the interviews following the match, Ali identified physical and emotional reasons for his loss (Rais, 2022). He knew exactly where he went wrong and lost the plot. Knowing when to admit defeat is a basic requirement of leadership, but understanding why the failure happened is what defines exceptional leaders. Some leadership coaches use an evidence-based approach to help their clients gain insight into the failure. DiSC assessments can be useful to get to the root of behavioral and personality traits. The DiSC assessment is a tool that assesses behavior. The resulting report includes an analysis of one's personality and advice on improving performance. After setbacks, it is advised to focus on two key areas of the assessment: values and attributes. By analyzing these areas, one can identify areas that need growth and development.

- **March to the beat of your drum**: Ali stayed true to himself. He was known for braggadocious comments, and many thought that his loss against Frazier would humble him. This was not the case! Ali accepted the loss confidently. His loss made for an incredible comeback story that remains relevant. Ali acknowledged that he had been beaten but maintained his charisma. He even joked around with reporters and deftly deflected questions that attempted to rub salt in his wounds. Failure is a tough thing to handle, but if we keep our wits about us, the journey to recovery becomes that much more tolerable.

- **Don't define yourself by your wins**: There is no denying that leaders are adored and respected when they are winning. This feeling of recognition can be so strong that leaders can have a hard time knowing how to handle failure. Ali handled his defeat like a champ because he controlled the narrative, using his defeat as a setup for his comeback story. Defeat did not intimidate or break Ali as he continued to train and compete, regaining the heavyweight title twice afterward. We can apply

Ali's singular focus to a world of stressful situations like this through

- *Taking care of your body and mind*: Physical and emotional health is intertwined in the web of well-being. Making time to improve our overall well-being and health is an investment that will pay dividends in every area of your life. Whether you set aside half an hour for meditation or are pursuing other health goals, it is the state of our well-being that largely dictates the quality of our lives.
- *Focusing on your leadership brand*: Your leadership brand has to do with your approach to leadership and your resulting reputation. Be intentional about managing your reputation, especially if failures threaten to upend your credibility as a leader.
- *Networking*: Hiding your head in the sand or keeping a low profile might sound like a natural reaction after a setback of loss, but it does you no favors. Meeting new people and forging relationships are essential to finding opportunities after a setback. So take the time to gain clarity on why the venture failed, and work on eliminating blind spots. Make that failure the first

chapter of a riveting comeback story, just like Ali did.

IDENTIFYING AS A LEADER

Self-identity is a big deal when it comes to leadership. Research shows that seeing yourself as a leader is a crucial first step on the path of leadership, whereas reluctance to identify as a leader can stunt growth and development (Cunningham et al., 2022). So why are people sometimes reluctant to see themselves as the leaders they were meant to be? No doubt that there are many factors contributing to this reluctance, but reputational concerns can play an overarching role in dissuading people from pursuing their goals. Three very specific reputational fears seem to play a dominant role in holding people back from leadership positions. These fears are the following:

Fear of Being Seen as Domineering

Many people are concerned about being seen as autocratic, bossy, or domineering when they don the mantle of leadership. These fears are often expressed in the words like, "I don't want to come across as pushy or bossy." There's good reason to be concerned about domineering and controlling personalities. In many instances, these personalities can trigger an escalation in conflicts, decrease trust, and stimulate ongoing bickering. For those who suspect they might have domineering tendencies, these tips will go a long way to create healthier work environments.

- *Soften the approach*: Watch your language, and keep in mind that there is a difference between demands and threats. When situations arise, explore them without allocating blame. Reflect on your feelings, and take ownership of it. At the end of the day, nobody is to blame for your feelings of anger, frustration, or elation. Only you can be responsible for your feelings.
- *Stimulate cooperation*: Cooperation is a give and take. We need to find common ground, welcome input, and work collaboratively to achieve success. Allocating tasks equally and listening to team members' concerns help to create a collaborative environment in which teams can deliver their best work.
- *Address your anxieties*: We all are likely familiar with the quote about worrying and rocking chairs. Stressing about our problems may be a natural reaction, but it is hardly a productive one. I've seen leaders become incapacitated by worry. Instead of worrying over possible worst-case scenarios, spend time exploring the source

of your anxiety instead. The goal is to uncover the roots of your anxiety without acting on it or projecting it onto others; most likely the source of your anxiety can be found in your history (Grover, 2017). Once a person has identified what triggers their need to exert control over others, steps can be taken toward controlling that impulse. Over time, these people notice that their relationships tend to improve dramatically.

Fear of Being Different

Another common concern that leaders harbor is that of being singled out and receiving too much attention for being different, even if that attention is a positive thing. Leaders might express these fears as, "I am comfortable leading, but I want to be on level-pegging with everyone else." Many times, those who assume leadership positions worry that they will need to sacrifice their sense of belonging within the group (Cunningham et al., 2022). They fail to realize that cultivating a culture of belonging starts with them! Eliminating the sense of *outsiderness* that exists in many groups can help, as people tend to suppress their unique attributes when they feel different from their colleagues. Feeling like an outsider can be a painful, negative experience. More than that, feeling like an outsider is a mental distraction that eats away at focus and performance. Keep in mind that the work environment will never be a one-size-fits-all situation. Respected leaders are aware of this and strive to instill a workplace culture that celebrates individuality, demonstrates care for team members, and provides opportunities for growth. Support, understanding, and trust are the essential ingredients needed to reduce feelings of outsiderness in the team.

Leaders can grow confident in their role by encouraging employees to value each other and advocating for everyone's voices to be heard. These leaders invest in their colleagues' development and actively try to build an inclusive workplace. Some leaders choose to show they care through benefits and initiatives.

Benefits, such as flexible work schedules, skills development programs, and wellness programs, signal our contemporaries and team members that we care about the distinct needs of individuals. These signs of appreciation can help to encourage a sense of belonging; in fact, benefits and initiatives can increase the sense of inclusion by up to 40% (Wiles & Turner, 2022).

Fear of Appearing Unfit for Leadership

Many potential leaders view themselves as unfit to take the helm. Some may feel uncomfortable embracing a role traditionally associated with male dominance, while others worry that their leadership will not be taken seriously. There are real experiences that often inform and stroke these fears, especially when we talk about underrepresented groups. These fears can have a significant impact on how we view ourselves and those around us. People who worry more over their reputation are less likely to be seen as leaders. From a psychological viewpoint, this result is not surprising. Leadership can come with pretty substantial changes. Some people choose to redefine their identities as a justification for avoiding the responsibility and weight that comes with leadership. It is more comfortable to rationalize an unwillingness to lead away, than to face judgment. The good news is that leadership is a skill. That means it can be learned and that tools exist to help hesitant individuals face their fears regarding leadership. Here are a few practical approaches to address that leadership fear:

- *Recognize weakness*: The first step in beating leadership anxiety is understanding one's weaknesses and strengths. Analyzing our strengths and weaknesses gives us a good understanding of the foundation we have to work with and where improvement is needed. For example, if you know that public speaking makes you sweat bullets, it might be a good idea to enroll in a public speaking course to help overcome the fear. When we know what our weaknesses are, it becomes easier to focus our energies on the solution.

- **Eliminate indecisiveness**: One of the basic requirements of leadership is decisiveness. That's because important, time-sensitive decisions will be made from time to time. Sometimes, the fear of making the wrong decisions can prove to be a significant stumbling block for leaders. Indecisiveness is many times a sign that a leader lacks confidence in themselves. Leaders need to trust their ability to make the right choices on time.
- **Be guided by goals**: Goals should guide leaders in all their undertakings. Maintaining practical objectives will significantly help reduce leadership fear. This can be done by reframing one's objectives, essentially giving yourself permission to believe new things and pursue new ideas. For example, if a leader wants to double sales in one year, they should start by setting small and attainable goals. They might

decide that the initial goal is to increase sales by 10% over the next 12 weeks. Successful achievement of this smaller goal helps to boost confidence in the leader and the team they are guiding.
- **Bolster your confidence**: Self-confidence is vital to overcoming fear in a leadership position. This confidence can be built by mingling with other successful leaders, seeking out a mentor, and educating oneself on leadership (Bates, 2018). Reading books or listening to podcasts on leadership can be especially effective when a new leader is trying to understand how others overcome the fears associated with leadership.

Keep in mind that no intervention will eliminate fears completely, but it can help to limit the negative impact thereof. Keep in mind that leadership is a very learnable skill, so some fears and uncertainty are natural, but it is nothing that can't be overcome. People who view leadership as a learnable skill tend to feel more comfortable with setbacks.

TRANSITIONING INTO LEADERSHIP

Taking those first tentative steps into a leadership role is a major milestone for anyone's career. Moving into a leadership position can bring with it a mixed bag of emotions: excitement, insecurity, fear, and anticipation. The goal for new leaders to successfully navigate the transition from team member to leader is to gain confidence in their leadership abilities. Leadership coaching and mentoring can prove extremely useful, but if you are not quite ready for that step yet, the strategies below can help to ease the transition.

Shifting Perspectives

Celebrate the trials and tribulations that got you to this point! Think about what you did in your former role and what your responsibilities are in the new one. Chances are there are some significant changes to perspective that need to take place. A little visualization exercise can help to drive this point home. Imagine that in your previous role, you were essentially sitting cross-legged on the ground, actively engaged in your work. Now that you've gained a new role, you are not on the same level anymore. You are viewing the work from a higher vantage point, which enables you to see things you didn't notice before. Think about what resources you have access to now. Reflect on what new work you need to do that you have not done before. Many new leaders fall into the trap of trying to fill two roles: the former one and the new one. Doing so is a recipe for disaster. Rather look for repeatable processes that you can create, and put in place to make the work manageable and consistent (Barrow, 2021).

Thought Before Action

Learning can feel overwhelming at times in a new role. When we have a long list of tasks screaming for our attention, it can be tempting to simply dive in and slough through them. One might presume that immediate action is the best way to stay productive, but this is not always the case. Action without thought beforehand is like sitting in a rocking chair: You won't be going anywhere. Rather err on the side of caution, pause, and evaluate before taking action. Informed decisions are the best way to go.

This reminds me of Stanley. He made a massive jump from being a mid-level manager to director. Naturally, he was feeling frustrated by the mountains of tasks he was expected to manage. Stanley had the habit of jumping straight into work, so I challenged him to create a new habit: thought before action. Instead of immediately slowly going through the list of tasks he had for the day, Stanley had to ponder different ways to approach the tasks. He had to determine what was the best way to use the resources he had at his disposal. As a result, Stanley managed to create consistent decision-making processes for himself which drastically reduced his frustration levels with the new position.

Practice Empathy

A challenge many new leaders face is learning how to communicate with team members and subordinates who used to be peers, especially if competition for the same position was tight. In these cases, "kill them with kindness" becomes apt advice. What I mean here is to disarm any dissent with candor and empathy. Then you take the helm like the leader you were meant to be.

A friend got a promotion and encountered a lot of pushback. She was in her 20s and suddenly became in charge of the team she used to work on. Competition for the leadership role was tough. Colleagues many years her senior applied for the job, so they were understandably upset (rebellious even) when a youngster was offered the role. The office became filled with gossip and grumbles. Instead of hiding away, she decided to face these facetious murmurings head-on. Calling a meeting with all her team members, she said something to the effect of, "I know many in this room have applied for this position. I am truly humbled that this opportunity was afforded to me. I know I'm young, but I'll do the best I can for all of you. My door is open if you need to discuss something in private with me." This honest conversation and open invitation helped to diffuse much of the tension that arose in the team.

Pay Attention to What Others Say

Starting a new role is exciting. We often wonder what we can do and change in our new roles. Before we get too caught up in the excitement of the moment, here's some sage advice: Pay attention to what others say, especially where the needs of leadership and the team are concerned. Ask yourself:

- What are leadership's goals and priorities?
- What stumbling blocks will prevent those goals and priorities from being realized?
- How can I assist in the process while holding the appropriate people accountable?

The answers to these questions will help new leaders uncover the areas that need urgent attention.

Develop Your Leadership Approach

There are as many different ways to lead as there are people. Leadership is more than the top-down, authoritative model that's been handed down since before Henry Ford's days. Leadership is a multifaceted diamond. Some leaders choose to be out in the fray and lead from the front. Others choose to let purpose guide their approach, leading their teams from within. New leaders are encouraged to ask themselves which leadership style they gravitate toward and which would serve them. Think about what other leadership approaches can be used in different scenarios. Don't be afraid to experiment a little to find out what works best; that is how we learn and grow in our roles as leaders.

Imagine gaining a new leadership role, only to be met with the frustration of a team member who won't follow your directions! This is what happened to me early in my leadership journey. The team member was resisting my directions for one simple reason: territory. Yes, people can get pretty territorial, especially if they feel someone is encroaching on their area of expertise. At the time, I was leading from the front, but I decided to flip the script. I asked my resistant team member to propose a plan and exercised my leadership powers in a collaborative manner. The difference between the team members was night and day. I was no longer encroaching on the area of expertise they felt privy to. Instead, I was empowering the team members to use their expertise to achieve a goal. Once that team member felt valued and empowered, the project became a cakewalk. Not only that, but our relationship improved as a result.

When you start a new chapter in any career, keep in mind that you have the opportunity to develop your brand as a leader. Don't be hesitant to show others who you truly are, and don't let perfectionism hold you back either. So many leaders have this erroneous idea that perfection is a requirement of success. It is not. Leaders make mistakes every day, but it is how they come back from those mistakes that will ultimately define them. As a leader, we never stop asking questions, and we are constantly growing.

DEVELOPING A LEADERSHIP MINDSET IN CURRENT TIMES

Patience and time are powerful tools, especially at this moment when it seems like the foundations of workplace culture are being questioned and leaders are trying to steer their ships toward a more peaceful horizon. Take a moment to reflect on the value of time in these cases. As companies surge toward the future on the wings of innovation, leaders are advised to remain cognizant of the weight and value that time bears, especially on the outlook of business thinking.

As leaders continue to explore the workplace of tomorrow and delve into the New Economy, leadership can take a page out of the Disability Economy's playbook to create more robust workplaces (Kaufman, 2022).

The mindset and ethos on which the Disability Economy rests are an inherent understanding.

Disability is part of the human experience; therefore, it is only a matter of time until someone experiences the effects of disability. A thorough understanding of this concept should, in theory, provide leadership in the Disability Economy with a suitable framework to face challenges.

We have seen firsthand how fast the world of work is changing. From the pandemic to the repercussions of generational needs, the agents of change seem to be working overtime. New buzzwords and terms seem to be popping up all the time. *Quiet quitting* certainly alarmed many when it emerged in business circles. Keep in mind though that expressions like these have existed in the past; our technology simply allows these sentiments to be amplified like never before. So it is up to leadership to recognize that change is natural and needs to happen and to respond to these changes.

Greater consideration can be given to the valuable tools leadership can gain through a greater appreciation of the Disability Economy, especially in the context of evolving work culture. Writer Sara Hendren describes the term *crip time* in one of her works. *Crip* is shorthand for "cripple," but the disability community reclaimed this term, turning it into a cultural representation instead of something derogatory. Hendren describes *crip time* as a flexible shorthand within the disability culture that is used for a range of uneasy situations that may arise in the work environment. One might need extra time to perform daily functions and therefore run on *crip time*. Some leaders are hesitant to afford their team members a measure of leeway, time, and freedom as this could impact their deadlines. In this sense, the term comes to describe how our environment and work demands are out of sync with our personal needs. This mismatched state is something leadership needs to think about, as finding ways to create bonds with team members and communities at large is a fundamental change agent to the future of work.

As leaders strive to create balance in an ever-changing work environment, the current times can be seen as a great asset. Leaders have the opportunity to stimulate a new era within the leadership sphere, one where the relationship between employee and employer is redefined. Developing a leadership mindset requires an honest evaluation of your skills. The purpose of this evaluation is to highlight strengths and weaknesses. Many turn to professional coaches or leadership assessments to help them in this process.

Big sweeping changes may not be everyone's cup of tea, so many leaders choose to take smaller steps. Set aside some time for introspection, evaluating yourself on the elements of a leadership mindset discussed above. Give yourself a score out of 10 for each element; this makes it easier to identify where to start improving. Improving on your shortcomings is a step that greatly improves the quality of leadership. To refine leadership further, we need to take responsibility for everything under our watch.

More on leadership responsibility in the next chapter.

AN EASY WAY TO WORK ON YOUR PEOPLE SKILLS IMMEDIATELY!

"No act of kindness, however small, is ever wasted."

— AESOP

We discussed soft skills, or people skills, at the beginning of the book – the skills needed to form connections with others. These are the skills you'll be using to unite your team around a common goal, and that's incredibly powerful.

Of course, these skills don't just come into play in your role as a leader – they're there throughout your entire life. They unite groups of friends working to achieve a common objective, a family working together to plan a vacation, a group of volunteers collectively raising money for a particular cause… and they have the potential to unite leaders from all over the world too.

Although the goals of your organization may look different from someone else's, there are big parallels between the aims of leaders everywhere. Each one wants to guide a happy, fulfilled, and productive team in taking their company to success. And those people skills aren't just useful within those teams – they're useful in helping leaders support and learn from each other too.

This is your opportunity to put those skills into practice – in the easiest way possible.

By leaving a review of this book on Amazon, you'll be helping other leaders find the information that will carry their organization to success.

All you have to do is take a few moments to tell new readers how this book has helped you and what they can expect to find inside… and they'll be pointed in the direction of the same guidance that will help them.

Thank you for your support. It's amazing how easy it is to create a community when everyone is working toward a common goal.

Scan the QR code below for a quick review!

4

LEADER RESPONSIBILITY

Millennials have had an interesting impact on leadership. We are currently in the middle of an ethically conscious awakening, a finding that is backed by research. A study found that ethics carries more weight than a generous salary as 62% of surveyed individuals noted that they wanted to work for an organization that made a difference (Jenkin, 2015). Millennials are an important generation for several reasons: They are the biggest group and are prepared to spend more money than the generation that came before. Compared to older consumers, millennials spend more on their weekly shopping for essentials as well. Millennials hold considerable spending power, which is why a change in attitude in leadership practices is vital. Leaders need to promote their values and ethics more than ever before as millennials can be quite choosy on where to spend their hard-earned greenbacks.

Ethics have fast become an important aspect of the recruitment process. It is becoming increasingly clear that young people want to work in organizations that make a difference, organizations that care, organizations that place renewed pressure on the leadership to attract new talent and maintain and grow existing customer bases. These leaders have to lead in a way that communicates social responsibility, but it can only be done if they have a good understanding of what responsible leadership entails.

Responsible Leadership Versus Greenwashing

Responsible leadership is about making sustainable decisions that take into account the interests of stakeholders. These stakeholders include shareholders, clients, employees, the community, suppliers, and future generations. There's a big difference between a genuine interest in making sustainable decisions and a symbolic gesture. Businesses are increasingly finding themselves facing compliance scandals. Whether it be in their own practices or those of their suppliers, greenwashing often rears its ugly head. Greenwashing happens when an organization markets itself as environmentally conscious but, in reality, isn't making any notable efforts. It's lip service, and leadership is to blame. A study conducted in Germany found that authoritarian leadership styles significantly impact sustainability behaviors, leading to an increase in greenwashing practices (Blome et al., 2017). The study also found that leadership styles that embrace ethics as a core value helped to prevent greenwashing from happening.

There are a lot of challenges that you'll face as a leader. Employees, students, team members, policymakers, and clients all demand different things from an organization. Each group brings with their unique concerns and needs, which means some tough decisions will lie ahead. Quick fixes won't do, as responsible leaders need to make decisions that satisfy two criteria:

- Are the decisions ethical?
- Were all relevant opinions considered in the decision-making?

Responsible leadership requires you to evaluate the questions you are asking concerning the way the organization operates. Leaders who can identify the barriers to responsible leadership stand a good chance of making positive, tangible changes. Ask these questions about your organization:

- Are business activities and operations sustainable?
- Are the employees looked after?
- Does the business take risks that can harm its reputation?
- If subcontractors are used, do their ethical practices line up with company policy?

In addition to evaluating the way an organization operates, responsible leaders will need to acquire some hard skills. One such example is understanding what sustainable practices entail to develop your professional value. Knowing how to engage with different stakeholders is also a key skill leaders will need to develop. Successful responsible leaders also possess an interesting mix of soft skills and personality traits that include honesty, empathy, respect, open-mindedness, having a long-term perspective, and a disposition of serving others (Nottingham Trent University, 2017).

OWNERSHIP: THE KEY TO BECOMING AN EXCEPTIONAL LEADER

Exceptional leadership is about taking ownership. Ownership is about being resolute, owning the consequences of your actions, solving problems, and withdrawing from liability. Ownership is the cornerstone of your sense of leadership and dictates the extent to which a person will step up and take initiative (VXI Marketing, 2021).

Leaders will face character-defining situations that can make or break their reputations. A leader who takes ownership does not easily give in to temptation. They understand that the right choice can be hard to make; therefore, the choice must be for the good of all. Leaders know how to delegate but don't blame others when the pawpaw hits the fan. They seek to understand the situation and strive to make an informed choice. Leaders who take ownership don't dwell on the problem and actively explore solutions. Taking ownership builds trust and support within teams and creates a culture of accountability.

When we consciously choose to take responsibility, there are four things we need to consider:

- **Who it is about**: Taking ownership is not about you. It is about everyone else. Corporate and organizational environments can be very competitive, and it can be tempting to diminish your involvement when failures arise. Consequently, some leaders hang their teams out to dry not realizing that the consequences of their actions are far-reaching. Team members might happily leave you to take the fall for mistakes, or they might hide things from you precipitating a new problem. Other times, teams might not trust their leader to take the proper corrective action, which can lead to problems of unforeseen scale. Any approach that eschews responsibility in favor of self-preservation is a no-win path to travel as a leader.

- ***People don't want to be coddled***: While it is true that your team is depending on you for guidance, it is important to keep in mind that people are smart and observant too. People can spot a half-truth or an attempt to deflect blame. People are quick to notice the signs of an untrustworthy leader and will react to the signals sent. Put yourself in an employee's shoes: When it comes to job security, you'd likely want any signal from your leader that tells them they are up to the task. You'd look for a leader who gives actionable ways to jump in and help, empowering you to solve problems. Employees notice everything and know when something is brewing. Downplaying a situation, coddling, or using team members as scapegoats is not doing anybody any favors. When worry arises, choose to head off their fears at the pass with a simple reassurance. Speak plainly, and don't take a circuitous route out of tough situations. In short, be the leader for your team that you would want to learn from yourself.

- *Don't play the blame game*: The truth is it does not matter whose fault it is when things go sideways, no matter how involved your role was, as the leader part of the responsibility will fall squarely on your shoulders. It comes with the territory. The leader's job is not to deny responsibility but to accept it loudly, visibly, and quickly. As soon as it's clear that there is a problem that is affecting the team or organization, the best route to earn trust is by accepting responsibility and owning the issue. New leaders should not shy away from taking responsibility as it can be an effective shortcut for demonstrating character and can help to secure buy-in from stakeholders (Conant, 2017). Own the problem, and fix it, no matter if there's a lot to blame to go around. This does not mean that people who contributed to the issue should not be held accountable. Hold responsible parties accountable, make the needed adjustments, and ensure that these mistakes won't repeat—that is the essence of ownership.

We are defined by our actions, not by the difficulties that we face. The goal of taking ownership of a situation is so that precrisis levels of productivity can be restored. Keep in mind that everybody has a lot on their plates, so learn from your mistakes and avoid comparing the present situation to events of the past. It is also best to refrain from reminding everyone constantly of what has happened. Doing so erodes the trust that teams have in their leaders. The next time you find yourself in a crisis, don't nitpick whose fault it was or try to deflect or underestimate the people around you. Own the problem, and take a hard-nosed approach where need be.

Ways Leaders Take Responsibility

When a leader is consistent in taking responsibility for their actions, they demonstrate dependable qualities. These individuals lead by example and are not afraid to make difficult decisions when needed. These leaders step up their leadership game in several ways:

- **They are involved in projects**: Responsible leaders are involved in projects. Even when they have a lot on their plate, these leaders will often take on small tasks that can be finished quickly. This demonstrates to the team that

they are invested in the project and willing to help.
- **They are accountable**: Accountable leaders know that everyone makes mistakes from time to time. These leaders do not play the blame game. Instead, they opt to jump into action to fix a problem as efficiently as possible. These leaders are not fazed by inconsistencies or failures and focus instead on helping their teams get through testing times.
- **They support their teams**: One of the quickest ways to spot unsupportive leadership is to take a look around the office. Signs of burnout and overly stressed staff are one of the earliest indicators that the team is not getting the support they need. Support your team and encourage them to take time off and rest if any of these red flags surface:

  - feeling tired most of the time
  - withdrawing from responsibilities
  - a loss of interest in work
  - increased levels of self-doubt or helplessness

Part of being a responsible leader is to keep an eye on your team's well-being. If you suspect team members are closing in on burnout, it becomes your duty to ensure that they get the rest that's needed. A rested team is a productive team.

- **They provide resources**: Making sure that your team has the resources they need to do the job right is both a priority and a responsibility. This could mean providing additional training or providing new tools and resources to assist them with their tasks. Provide your team with the necessary information, or develop their skills with mentors and coaches. Whatever the case may be, equipping your team with the resources they need to succeed is the responsibility of every leader. Don't be afraid to ask your team if there's anything they need to help them be more successful at their job.
- **They remain engaged**: It is easy to shrug off a problem and pass the buck. Responsible leaders know that this is a luxury they do not have. Instead, they are open-minded and offer help where needed. Engagement comes in many shapes and sizes. As long as leaders show a willingness to help, the people around them will take note. It can do wonders for employee and team morale. Great leaders have sworn by the transformative power of one-on-ones for

decades. A study found that employees who got little one-on-one time with their leader were far more likely to be disengaged. The same study pointed out that employees who received twice the number of one-on-ones with their leader, relative to their peers, are 67% less likely to be disengaged (Fuller & Shikaloff, 2016). When a leader doesn't meet with team members or employees at all, they are four times as likely to be disengaged and twice as likely to view leadership unfavorably (Calvello, 2022). Making time for your team, whether it is one-on-one or simple troubleshooting, makes a big difference in the long run.

LEADERSHIP LESSONS FROM HISTORY

Many of us are familiar with Henry Ford and the Model T car. The success story is often used to demonstrate what it takes to be a leader in terms of persistence, creative thinking, and hard work. There's no doubt that these qualities are shared among leaders, but the focus on Ford's success often overshadows and cheapens the lessons we can learn from his failures.

The earliest automobiles were made by hand and were expensive. This meant that only the rich could afford to buy a car. Things changed dramatically for the transportation industry on October 1, 1908, when the first Model T rolled off the assembly line. The assembly line rapidly became synonymous with Ford's ingenuity, making the Model T one of the first affordable cars aimed at the mass market. In seven years, Ford managed to sell a million Model Ts, doubling the number in the following year and a half. Over the next 25 years, Ford had one of the most successful automobile companies globally, granting him the title of America's second billionaire (John D. Rockefeller being the first one). This is the Ford success story that most of us are familiar with: the visionary who changed an entire industry through persistence, hard work, and sheer tenacity. But those who are familiar with Ford's story on a deeper level know that the company was on the brink of bankruptcy.

During the 1920s, the Model T's dominance in the market was failing. Subtle but sure trends emerged that tilted the scales of dominance away from the automobile manufacturer, but Ford stuck to his assembly line and mass production concept regardless. Things were changing impressively fast. By 1920, roughly half the American population lived in cities. The working class could finally enjoy more leisure time, and some companies ventured to implement the two-week vacation policy. Hollywood captured Americans' imaginations with motion pictures. Sporting events drew excited crowds (especially Babe Ruth's legendary game in 1927). Popular culture and all its trappings of style, fashion, and culture have arrived in the United States.

The Bubble Trap: A Leader's Downfall

Nearly a century later, the advent of pop culture may not seem like such a big deal, but keep in mind it is a strong force. Pop culture primarily builds and strengthens our interactions with people who are into the same things. One example of how pop culture manifests itself in our modern society is through Comic-Con. Every year, the event brings people with a shared interest in comic books, cosplay, film, science fiction, games, and anime together.

Pop culture was quite the social transformation that also affected the car industry. Automobiles were originally considered to be mechanical horses, a means of transportation. Soon enough, vehicles became a status symbol for the wealthy. Automobiles had one characteristic that enabled this change: They were mobile advertisements of status. Most of our possessions are not on display, and it is considered rude to ask about someone's financial assets. The only way anyone could guess at your level of wealth is if that person was invited to your home. The automobile, however, is on display whenever and wherever you drive making it a visible, mobile status advertisement, a phenomenon that is observable in many countries around the world today. As a result, motor vehicles became more popular than before, but Henry Ford did believe automobiles are anything more than appliances (Vakil, 2019). This belief was visible in the Model T factory.

The factory and the way the Model T was produced had remained the same for several years. Even the pricing structure remained unchanged. The Model T was only available in black and did not take into consideration how consumer expectations were changing during the 20s. Even though the car market kept growing rapidly, Ford's sales were relatively flat in 1925 when compared to sales of the previous year. Ford's market share plummeted from a dominating 54% to a worrisome 45% in a short time. It was a clear sign of danger, but Ford was not paying attention to these red flags. He had fallen victim to *the bubble trap* just like many other successful leaders.

As it happens with many successful leaders, Henry Ford chose to ignore the signs of changing times. He sheltered himself from reality in a neat little bubble, surrounded by yes-men. Ford's little bubble helped to create the conditions for his competition to flourish. General Motors seized the opportunity and offered what the customers wanted: vehicles as status symbols. They offered different colors and models of cars and listened to feedback. General Motors went a step further and introduced a yearly model change for all their car lines. With the yearly model change, vehicles were solidified as a status symbol which set the tone for General Motors to flourish in the coming decades. The world of motoring would be a very different place had Ford been willing to listen and adapt.

The Slipping Clutch of Leadership

A slipping clutch is a relatively common and frustrating problem with manual vehicles. When the clutch slips, the engine cannot deliver power to the wheels, and as a result, the vehicle will not move. Slipping clutches are normally caused by driving and vehicle quality. If you find yourself favoring fast acceleration and aggressive gear changing, you may find that the clutch will give out sooner than it is supposed to. Similarly, skipping the service on your vehicle will cause damage to the clutch over time, leading it to slip. In much the same way, leadership operates in the same way. If the leader at the helm fails to empower and support their teams, no progress can be made. They'll be stuck in the driveway. Similarly, if leaders find themselves favoring hastily made plans or ignoring valuable feedback, they will need to take a deep introspective look into the quality of their leadership. By being comfortably nestled in his bubble,

Ford did not realize that the clutch was slipping on his leadership.

Some of the first signs of troubled waters came when the sales department had to inform Ford that Model T sales were falling. Sales fell so badly that the department feared Model T sales would stop soon if no drastic changes were made. Ford allegedly dismissed the problem and painted the sales department unfavorably. It would seem that Ford was not ready to adapt to changing times. One brave soul who dared to *bell the cat* wrote a seven-page memorandum, delivering it to Ford in 1926. The man was Ernest Kanzler. He laid the unpleasant truth bare in those seven pages. His reward was the same as many others who gave unfavorable feedback. Kanzler was fired.

There was irrefutable evidence that Ford's strategy was failing, yet later in 1926, he announced that their vehicles will still be made in the same way. Had Ford realized that the bubble trap and his denial of reality would keep him in General Motors' shadow for the next eight decades, he surely would have changed his leadership style.

Ford's innovation on Ransom E. Olds' assembly line concept helped to improve the production of automobiles. His tenacity and drive to succeed are commendable, but ultimately, it was the lack of people skills that was his downfall. Keep in mind that every leader can fall prey to bad leadership habits. The biggest culprit? The bubble trap. The bubble trap creates an environment of constant positive reinforcement (courtesy of yes-men) that strengthens bad leadership habits. Responsibility and accountability are two sides of the same leadership coin. Venture with me into the next chapter as we explore how accountability creates balanced and fair leaders.

5

LEADER ACCOUNTABILITY

Be accountable for every failure and success. When we accept responsibility for our actions and are willing to own the outcomes of our choices, decisions, and actions, we are accountable. The majority of leaders understand the value of leadership accountability, yet in practice, many fail to deliver.

A global survey revealed interesting insights that leadership accountability had on the performance of a company. Over 2,000 human resources and senior executives took part in the survey. The results revealed that two thirds of the participants felt that leadership accountability was a crucial issue in their company (Routley, 2020). Only one third of the participants were happy with the levels of accountability demonstrated in their companies. When the survey responses were sorted into three categories, interesting trends emerged. The three categories were low performers, average performers, and industry leaders. Of those categories, *industry leaders* had the most interesting results.

Those who fell in the *industry leader* category were twice as likely to have clear expectations for their leadership. They were also more likely to identify high-potential leaders, embrace diverse thinking, and implement development programs to build the capacity of their teams. Furthermore, leadership teams from these companies were far more likely to understand their target market and trends affecting the business, demonstrate emotional intelligence, and embrace a passion for executing the company vision.

Building a strong leadership culture starts with asking some tough questions. The first step would be to assess what you, your team, and your organization are doing. Reflect on the following:

- Did the company or team set clear leadership expectations?
- Are individuals in leadership roles committed and capable of handling their tasks?
- Is there a strong leadership culture in the company?

- Is mediocre leadership identified and addressed at all levels?

If you answered *no* to any of the questions above, it means there's some work that needs to be done. Treat it as an opportunity to develop an effective and accountable team. The outcomes might pleasantly surprise you.

Accountability Leads to Quality Outcomes

Team members and employees are far more likely to trust leaders who demonstrate accountability. When we are willing to own the outcomes of our choices, we instill confidence in our team members. It creates a culture of accountability. There are many benefits to creating a high-trust environment. Compared to individuals in low-trust environments, people in high-trust environments have been found to experience less stress, more energy, fewer sick days, increased productivity, and a 76% in engagement (Zak, 2017). A meta-analysis of decades' worth of data revealed that high engagement rates consistently lead to positive outcomes (Harter et al., 2016). Other benefits of high-trust environments include the following:

- ***Strengthening relationships***: Stronger relationships are a happy side effect of high-trust environments. When team members and employees feel like they can have an open, engaged conversation with their leaders, they are far more likely to be engaged. These teams are far more likely to share feedback or ask questions in general, which can lead to quality outcomes. Studies found that organizations with high-trust environments experience 2.3 times greater revenue growth than organizations that don't have high-trust environments (Rath, 2018).

- *Reducing costly mistakes*: When we own up to our mistakes, we can more easily find a solution and move on. Recall Ford's story in the previous chapter. Many of the problems he faced were exacerbated by a lack of accountability on his behalf. Keep in mind that accountability is the glue that holds successful teams together.

Mentoring and leadership coaching are very effective at strengthening the muscle of accountability (Torch, 2021). A study by the Association for Talent Development confirms this as well. They found that people have a much higher chance of completing a goal if they commit to someone, like a mentor or leadership coach (Oppong, 2017). Mentors and coaches play a supporting role in various aspects of accountability.

They can help to improve a leader's accountability by identifying key areas that need to be worked on. Accountability is a vital trait that everyone in a leadership position needs to demonstrate.

Hold Yourself Accountable

Accountability is critical for success, at least that's what 72% of business leaders and human resources professionals think (Harrison, 2017). Ignoring accountability creates a breeding ground for problems, including resentment among team members and fractured trust. In some cases, team members could feel less aligned with company values, which may lead them to seek opportunities elsewhere. There's no getting around it. Ignoring accountability sets a poor example. Evaluate your level of accountability by reflecting on the following:

- When faced with an issue, are you willing to accept responsibility?
- If you have accepted that something is your fault, do you add excuses?
- Are you quite willing to say, "I don't know," when you don't have the answer to a question?

Your level of accountability will depend on your answers. The good news is that everyone can improve their ability to hold themselves accountable with the tips below.

- **Be mindful of your language**: Language is a big signal of whether we are holding ourselves accountable or not. When we find ourselves evading ownership, it is a good idea to take stock and work toward fixing that behavior. Make a conscious effort to use words and a tone that communicates the intent of ownership.
- **Be honest**: Leaders are not meant to have all the answers. It is fine to make mistakes. Learn from your mistakes and grow as a leader.
- **Work to solve the issue**: Once you've taken responsibility for your mistakes, resist the temptation to ask someone else to come up with the solution. Being accountable means seeing the job through to the end, especially when we experience failures.
- **Consider what is best for the group**: Effective leaders know that true success can only be obtained when the group is doing well. Success is a group effort.
- **Own your role**: Leaders who are intimidated to lead or are afraid of getting things wrong tend to shirk accountability as well. Individuals who

find themselves in leadership positions need to own their role or risk becoming a shadow in the background. Leaders who own their roles are willing to make hard decisions and admit to their mistakes.

Fear is often the reason why some shy away from accountability (Price, n.d.). It is a fear of judgment or reprimand that comes with our mistakes. It can be hard to escape feeling forgetful or incompetent after a blunder. Our culture has a lot to answer for here. We are taught from kindergarten days to associate failure with something bad. The truth is failure is necessary. People learn from their mistakes, and when we challenge ourselves, we develop our abilities. Keep in mind that it is not our mistakes that define us but how we react to those mistakes. Great leaders own up to their mistakes and embrace it as a relatable learning experience.

DEMONSTRATING ACCOUNTABILITY

A lack of accountability often comes with a high cost where problems could snowball. So how does one remedy the situation if you find yourself in a low-accountability environment? As with many things, before looking at how to embed accountability into your team or workplace culture, leaders need to reflect if they are demonstrating accountability. Ask yourself:

Are the Goals and Targets Unclear?

Unclear goals and targets are a guaranteed way of creating frustration in the team. Leadership accountability and a culture of accountability cannot exist if you don't know what you are supposed to be accountable for. Leaders need to set clear goals for their teams to be successful. Goals need to be measurable and meaningful if they are to help a team succeed. Take the time to evaluate if goals are specific, measurable, achievable, realistic, and time-bound (Matusky, 2021). If the goals are not, they need to be reworked to be made transparent.

Are You Future-Focused?

Accountable leaders can take a challenging vision and make it a reality. They conquer these mountainous challenges one step at a time. These steps are arranged in chronological order, and checklists with clear deliverables are assigned. Through regular reviews, the team is held accountable. Most importantly, wins are celebrated along the way. An accountable leader does not shy away from the question, "how do we get from point A to B?" Instead, that leader realizes that they are shouldering a responsibility toward their team: the need to provide clarity on how their team can excel and achieve goals.

Do You Ask for Help?

Even though accountable leaders strive to create clear goals and targets, challenges are inevitable. Changes in the market, organization, or team will create new challenges, opportunities, and constraints. Many leaders are proud and choose to forge on. These leaders mistakenly believe that asking for help is a sign of weak leadership. In my experience, I found the opposite to be true. Accountable leaders don't let their pride get in the way, nor do they consider asking for help a weakness. These leaders know that when we ask for help, we are showing our team that we are committed and involved. This builds trust, which in turn helps teams and leaders achieve goals.

Do You Give Honest Feedback?

Leaders allow other members of the team to be accountable. The best way to do this is with constructive and honest feedback. Feedback is necessary as it lets the team know how they are performing, provides learning opportunities, and can help to achieve results. Confirming with a team member that their work is falling short of expectations, or is hitting the mark, is helpful. Constructive feedback takes this communication to the next level by helping the team with strategies for improvement and development. Many leaders wait until the performance review to give feedback to their teams, but this is a mistake. Often, by the time the performance review comes around, it is too late to address certain problems. Strive to provide constructive feedback in the moment. Treating constructive feedback is a continuous process. Doing so keeps the team in the loop when they need to change strategies. A leader who regularly provides constructive feedback to the team essentially allows everyone to be accountable.

Accountability Versus Responsibility

These terms are sometimes confused with each other, but there is a distinct difference that leaders should take note of. Responsibility is used with tasks and projects. Being responsible for something means that one should carry out these tasks. Responsibility can be shared, as in the case of teams that are collectively responsible for a required outcome. Responsibility is also a self-managed choice, meaning that one chooses to accept responsibility and it cannot be forced.

Accountability concerns itself with the consequences of one's actions. Accountability differs from responsibility on another level: the number of people it involves. Responsibility can be shared over a group, but accountability is often confused to select individuals. A blame game often ensues when accountability is shared in a group. Even when several people are responsible for a task, typically only one group member would be accountable for the consequences. If something goes wrong, the accountable individual must be able to relay what happened. If there is any need to make adjustments for negative consequences, the accountable person will be asked to do so. That accountable person is a leader. In short, responsibility relates to completing a task, whereas accountability relates to the consequences thereof. It is possible to be both accountable and responsible, but generally, accountability is reserved for leadership roles. Accountability is necessary. It ensures that leaders are doing their jobs.

When we think of a business, the leaders are usually removed from the day-to-day operations of the company. Instead, they are tasked with ensuring the business is profitable, satisfies shareholders, and maintains a good reputation among other duties. In the case of large corporations, mistakes can cost thousands of people their livelihoods, but only the company leadership is held accountable. Let's say the CEO of a company resigned because faulty goods were being distributed. The CEO has a responsibility to ensure that the goods are being produced according to the company guidelines and quality assurance standards. So if the production line produces faulty goods, the

CEO is accountable. Other things leaders and managers might be held accountable for include

- maintaining ethics and company culture
- meeting performance targets and satisfying shareholders
- maintaining a healthy work environment to keep employees happy and productive
- ensuring profitability and lowering expenses where possible

In any line of work, mistakes are a guarantee. Often, these mistakes are easy to address. Sometimes they are nightmarish scenarios affecting other people as well. If a company's actions had negative consequences for uninvolved parties, the affected persons may be entitled to compensation (Indeed Editorial Team, 2021b). This could be a result of legal action or form part of company policy. Determining who is responsible is not always easy. Let's look at the construction site for example. If a building was constructed, then found to be in breach of building regulations, who is responsible? It could be the architect, tradespeople, civil engineer, or a combination of everyone that was involved. Holding everyone accountable would be impractical, so it falls to the project manager. The manager would be expected to address the problems or resign in some cases. This is part of the reason why leadership positions come with fair compensation, as they are often held accountable for mistakes.

Building a Culture of Accountability

When companies and teams lack a culture of accountability, it can spell doom, especially for those in high-growth environments that are working on employee engagement and retention. A strong accountability culture means that leaders can trust their team and employees to deliver their best work. Establishing accountability in the workplace starts with

- considering how employees demonstrate accountability in their roles
- ensuring that staff takes ownership of the duties linked to their roles

After determining the levels of accountability, consider implementing the steps below to get a culture of accountability started.

Step One: Set Clear Expectations

Before presenting any expectations of accountability and ownership to a team or employees, leaders should narrow down their list of expectations. That's because these expectations will become standards that involve many stakeholders. When employees and team members have a clear picture of the company objectives and the standards to which they are held accountable, they will experience less stress. It may be helpful to present examples of accountability that act as a FAQ for current standards and goals.

When setting goals, try to be specific. For example, setting a goal to *increase sales from last year* is too broad and leaves a lot to the imagination. A goal that states, "to double sales on the West Coast by gaining significant market share from our competitors," is a lot more specific and tangible. Goals need to be realistic though. Lofty goals can discourage team members and communicate a message that the leadership is out of touch. Furthermore, goals should challenge employees just enough to drive performance. Another way leaders can instill accountability in team members and staff is through the use of deadlines. The use of deadlines should be reasonable and provide staff with enough time to perform their duties.

Step Two: Familiarize New Faces With the Accountability Culture

People make businesses work. Employees are the heartbeat of a company. Without them, a company turns into a soulless husk of brick and mortar. That's why it is vital to communicate your definition of ownership to employees from the very first day they become part of the team. Discuss the relationship between accountability and freedom at work from the very first day. This helps employees become self-directed and autonomous.

Increasing accountability in the workplace starts with the recruiting process. Leaders should only hire employees or select team members who are a good fit for the role. It would benefit them to look into where the recruit is coming from and what past employers had to say. During the hiring process, share with new recruits relevant accountability examples. This will help to make it clear to newcomers how to take ownership in their new environment. When explaining how recruits will be held to company standards, take note of their questions. By paying attention to their questions, leaders can address knowledge gaps to ensure that absolute clarity exists concerning standards and employee accountability.

Recruiting can be a costly process, so by focusing on accountability in this stage already, leaders are ensuring that they recruit individuals who will perform at a high level.

Step Three: Nip Accountability Issues in the Bud

Addressing the elephants in the room is the best way to create a culture of accountability and responsibility. To maintain accountability standards, it is advised to have clear criteria to coach team members and employees when they slip up. Always strive to provide examples of what accountability and success look like. Correcting staff and your team may feel awkward at first, but it is an important part of freedom and accountability in the work environment. It is important to nip any behavior that violates company policy and accountability standards in the bud.

When correcting team members and employees, the goal should be to coach. Never berate or embarrass the person you are correcting. It is demotivating and can create feelings of lingering resentment. When correcting through coaching, offer team members regular private reviews. Treat those short meetings like a miniature job performance review, and approach it with the intention to help the person excel in their role.

Should you discover that multiple team members are unsure of what is expected of them, a team meeting should be called. In this meeting, team members should be given the opportunity to learn their leader's employee accountability policy, be encouraged to take initiative at work, and voice any concerns that they may have. Team meetings are a wonderful tool to take the spotlight off of one individual and build a sense of unity. Leaders are encouraged to take the time to go over expectations and provide examples of ownership at work. Address team members' ideas and questions, and you'll be well on your way to creating a culture of accountability.

Making sure that everyone is on the same page is vital to earning the respect of your team. This respect should be visible in the job accountability examples that leaders use. Keep in mind that mentoring team members professionally and respectfully is highly effective at letting team members know they play an important part. Over time, this leads to a more solid accountability culture.

6

MASTERY OF SELF—THE DISCIPLINED LEADER

Mastering your habits is the key to becoming a successful and disciplined leader. Self-discipline is one of the most important foundational skills leaders need to develop early on. Let's be honest, for most leaders, self-discipline is a work in progress that's been wrapped in good intentions and procrastination. It does not have to be like that, though. Self-discipline, just like any other aspect of leadership, takes practice. Simply put, self-discipline is the ability to exercise self-control and to do what you should be doing. Self-discipline often involves a measure of sacrifice, putting off your immediate comfort or desires to achieve long-term success.

Humans are emotional beings. Our emotions, for better or worse, heavily influence our decision-making. The good news is that you already are the person you want to be. It is the emotional mind that needs to be reined in with self-discipline to propel growth. Having an emotional mind can be compared to having a pet: You are not directly in control of the pet's behavior, but you are still held responsible for it. As such, it becomes necessary to learn how to manage the emotional mind, as it has the power to impact our quality of life, decisions, and behaviors (Peters, 2013). Nurturing self-discipline is advantageous in a personal and professional capacity. It helps us to

- *Improve grit*: Grit is a positive trait that is associated with perseverance and passion. Self-discipline helps people to achieve difficult goals through sustained and focused efforts over time (Duckworth et al., 2007).
- *Reduce anxiety*: It is not uncommon to turn to vices when we feel stressed. We all have vices we turn to. Some procrastinate when stressed. Others play computer games or binge-watch series. These behaviors are an attempt to distract ourselves from the negative emotions we experience when stressed. A 2016 study found that improving self-control can help to reduce anxiety-related problems (Bertrams et al., 2016).

- ***Improve physical health***: People who regularly practice self-discipline are generally better able to resist health-damaging activities. A study in Taiwan proved this with an interesting experiment. The experiment rested on the assumption that if a smoker thinks abstractly, they will smoke less. The science behind it rests on the construal level theory, which suggests that high-level construal promotes self-control (Chiou et al., 2013). Simply put, if we focus on our goal instead of means and resources, our self-control improves. Byron Pulsifer, a motivational seminar leader, said it best: "Stay focused and don't allow distractions to fill your mind or derail you from taking continued action."
- ***Improve soft skills***: Self-control helps us to keep automatic defensive reactions in check (Heshmat, 2016). When we are less defensive, we can become more open-minded.
- ***Improve resilience***: The more resilient you are, the easier you'll be able to bounce back from adverse events. Self-discipline was found to be the key, as it helps us to exercise better control over our impulses. Resilient people have a strong belief in their abilities to overcome challenges (Prater, 2019).

Mastery over self helps us to take important actions, avoid harmful situations, and maintain necessary habits. Self-discipline is necessary to become a responsible and accountable leader. It is a critical skill because you won't always feel like doing what needs to be done. We all have those days. As any exceptional leader can tell you, there will be times when leaders need to make unpopular choices. Self-discipline helps these leaders make tough choices, because they need to model the behavior that their team will follow. They are self-disciplined because they want their teams to be consistent, reliable, and hardworking (Boxx, 2021).

DEVELOPING SELF-DISCIPLINE

Developing self-discipline means creating new habits. Disciplined leaders will often tell you that self-care is important. Keeping you and your body in good condition is not being selfish; it is about being the best you can be. Those who engage in self-care look after their body and mind through diet, exercise, and mind management. Our thoughts, whether they are positive or negative, exert a considerable influence on our lives. Disciplined leaders realize that self-care is not about becoming stoic but about acknowledging and understanding your emotions. Other habits that self-disciplined leaders develop include

- ***Respecting time***: Time is precious for everyone. Disciplined leaders live by the unspoken rule of never keeping someone waiting on them. They show up on time and honor deadlines. Time is precious, so it's always a good idea to make a habit of examining how you are using it.
- ***Controlling their thoughts***: The poet, Sylvia Plath, wrote a poem in which she explored the power words held over a life, likening it to a weapon. Through this poem, Plath illustrates that we can be our own worst enemies or our own best friends. Plath, unfortunately, ended her life in 1963; she was 30. The poem was titled *Words*. Disciplined leaders realize that their thoughts can impact how their day goes. Instead of being ruled by unwanted thoughts, they have boundaries in place. They actively choose to see the bright side of a bad situation. Furthermore, they do not allow others to manipulate their thoughts. You are the master of your thoughts, not the other way around.
- ***Focusing on the important things***: It is hard to maintain focus if you don't know what is coming next. This is why many leaders choose to plan out their day. This helps them to zoom in on important activities and boosts productivity.

- **Priding themselves on clear communication**: Let's be honest, when a leader can't communicate clearly, they set themselves and those around them up for failure. Highly disciplined leaders know that clear communication is the key to effective leadership.
- **Being committed**: Discipline and commitment are inseparable. You can't become disciplined without being committed. Commitment is what sees us following through on our choices, building discipline in turn.
- **Rewarding themselves**: The leadership journey is a long and hard one. As you work toward becoming more disciplined, obstacles will cross your path. It is not easy to deal with these obstacles, but rewarding yourself afterward helps to make it worthwhile. It also reduces the risk of becoming discouraged.

Helpful Hints to Develop Leadership Discipline

There's no denying that leaders have a tough job! They are expected to manage themselves, lead others, and keep things going in the right direction. With this comes a lot of stress and uncertainty that can interfere with leadership discipline.

I've had the pleasure to witness the wins of fantastic leaders. With that, I've seen the personal struggles, issues, and frustration that leaders endure. The leaders who embraced a disciplined approach experienced less frustration and higher levels of success. Using a checklist of disciplines can make this process easier. An outline can be found below.

Personal Disciplines

- *Identify your leadership principles*: Ask yourself what principles guide your leadership style. Think of four principles, and write them down. These should be personalized and nongeneric.
- *Communicate your expectations*: This step alone can reduce so much frustration! Leaders should identify and communicate the top three expectations that they have for each project or goal.
- *Be consistent*: Inconsistency only adds to stress and increases problems in the long run.
- *Excel*: High-level performance helps to grow discipline.

Work Discipline

- *Have a plan*: Most organizations and teams don't have a strategy. Strategies are an

opportunity to demonstrate the value that you bring as a leader. It creates uniqueness in the marketplace and identifies core competencies that can greatly assist leadership.
- ***Establish routine***: Routine creates discipline. The routine I'm talking about here is a set of meetings and communications. It is advisable to start with an annual strategic planning meeting. From there, we can add quarterly strategy updates, followed by monthly goal updates and weekly information meetings.
- ***Be team-centric***: The annual review process is a dated practice, and some leaders choose to implement a quarterly employee development plan instead (Gulledge, 2018). The development plan was presented as a self-assessment, and a set time was set aside for employee development.

What Discipline Looks Like

Disciplined leaders can be identified by their behaviors. These people tend to express self-discipline in interesting ways, and we can use these signs to spot disciplined leaders.

- ***They are in control of their moods***: These individuals do not allow their emotions to

cloud their judgment and live by their commitments.
- **They watch their words**: These leaders don't jump to conclusions and put their minds into gear before speaking. They restrain their reactions and strive to keep their cool, even in tense situations. These leaders understand that a short temper is detrimental to healthy leadership.
- **They stick to their schedule**: Time management skills are a boon for every leader and separate high performers from the rest. These leaders understand that you need to manage time efficiently to remain productive and excel.
- **They are good examples**: These individuals learn to live within their means and maintain their health by forming healthy habits.

A DISCIPLINED LEADER IN THE DIGITAL AGE

Leadership is about consistency and routine. It demands of us to actively work on our discipline until it feels like a natural part of working. Add to this the fast-changing nature of the digital age, and it becomes clear why discipline is crucial. When examining the habits of successful leaders in the digital age, focus on how they approach the following:

Creating High-Performance Environments That Encourage Success

Grasping the role of a leader in the digital age is the starting point for success. Bear in mind that it can be easy to mistake the digital world for something that is exclusively focused on technology. Technology still needs human input to function as it should. This makes the digital world about people, mindsets, and behaviors and how technology is used to create new ways of working and value propositions. Automation of work and digital disruption of business models demand of leaders to act on change quickly and effectively and with the least cost. Take a look at the metaverse as an example. Big tech did not waste any time getting behind the new technology. In 2021, Roblox announced its first metaverse music festival and has had numerous events since—all because they were quick to recognize the potential in their changing environment.

The role of a leader in today's world should be focused on creating an environment where success is a given. In this high-performance environment, leadership teams can challenge themselves and develop into stronger leaders.

Awakening Latent Potential in People

The energy you bring with you to work can influence how others react. We've all probably met a person who brightened up a room on entry. These people can light up rooms because they bring a positive mindset with them. You'll need that positive mindset to spot and awaken the potential in people. Leadership is concerned with understanding people and building trust. It is about building confidence and encouraging your team to excel.

Many times the action of managers and leaders can destroy confidence, leading to a disengaged and poorly performing team. We need to flip that script and start focusing on making teams feel safe and supported. Some leaders choose to coach for high performance to awaken the latent potential in their teams. In the end, it is all about developing people and helping them grow.

Operating Simply and Speedily

Clarity about the role and the purpose of leadership is necessary if one is to operate at the pace our modern world demands. Making decisions and moving forward is a great way to remove the fear, anxiety, and stagnation of uncertain times. Having a set of principles and adhering to them makes this a lot easier to pull off.

Remaining Authentic

When we understand ourselves and the story we have to tell, we can develop an authentic leadership style. This brand of leadership is based on our strengths and requires that we are comfortable with being vulnerable and confident in our abilities. It is about creating an environment where your team can trust you as a leader. The team should understand you and where you are coming from and follow your philosophy willingly. This only happens when leaders are themselves. Start to build on your self-awareness by examining your strengths and ensuring you are building on them.

Inspiring Action

Action without purpose is a waste of time. Purpose should be the center of everything that we do, doubly so as leaders. Inspiring action rests heavily on a leader's ability to communicate the meaning behind vision and strategy. Successful leaders can take a complex situation and use it to inspire action. It is all about creating a culture that can deliver the results we are looking for. To achieve this, leaders need the skills that will encourage people to willingly take action. Some of these skills include

- the ability to have constructive dialogue
- a leader's ability to tell stories

- the ability to effectively use metaphors
- fully engaging people while communicating

Exceptional leaders are best described as *purpose maximizers*. They create a tangible sense of value while providing direction and flexibility. These leaders create effective ways for everyone in their teams to make decisions easily, without needing authorization.

Developing High-Performance Teams

Our modern world is a fast-changing beast. If we want to maximize opportunities, we need to stay in touch with the times or be left behind. This is where high-performance teams make all the difference. There is an increasing call for leaders to create virtual, remote, global, and cross-functional teams relatively quickly. To do this, leaders will need to become comfortable with collaboration, autonomy, and empowerment quickly. There's a lot of ambiguity and complexity in today's world, necessitating the need to have diverse thinking teams, alliances, and partnerships. All require a good measure of skill and experience to create quickly and efficiently.

We do our teams a disservice when we focus only on results. If leaders focus on results but neglect to enable their team to achieve those, the team's performance will be strangled. In this case, the team is reduced to a collection of *attendees*. They are not the highly engaged team one would expect them to be. The problem can often be traced to an absent team-building strategy. Keep in mind that it falls to the leader to develop a self-managed team. In other words, develop your team so that there is no need for you to be around. That's how leaders open the doors of opportunity and promotion for themselves. Think about it for a minute: A leader is less likely to be promoted if the team's performance suffers as a result. Highly engaged teams are less likely to suffer a performance loss in the absence of their leader.

Embracing Innovation

The culture we create dictates the direction a team will move. Leaders should strive to create a culture that encourages individuals to come up with suggestions to improve performance. This adds value. There are opportunities to innovate in every aspect of business, but you need to be willing to try new things. Innovative leaders are comfortable with the risk of failure.

Navigating an Unfamiliar Terrain

Mental fortitude and resilience are must-haves for modern leadership. Today's leaders need to simplify the complex, be agile, understand the need for change, and be comfortable with paradoxes. Leaders are expected to anticipate risk. Not all risk is a bad thing though. Calculated risks can help to drive innovation, uncovering new ways of working. Early action and effective governance are key.

Teaching People

Leaders have a responsibility to help their team members adapt to change. To do this, leaders must inspire curiosity, encourage learning, and remain agile. Keep in mind that all change starts with changing mindsets. The digital age places a premium on learning, and leaders have to embrace this if they want to accelerate organizational growth.

Delivering Timely

As leaders, we need to join the dots, translate strategy into something meaningful, and adjust our work pace to honor deadlines. Simplicity is key here. As leader, you need to ensure that your purpose, goals, and plans are in alignment with your values. In a time-pressured environment, it can be easy to miss key steps along the way. Sometimes we are tempted to jump straight to the execution of a task in the interest of deadlines. When doing this, we run the risk of losing clarity. Without clarity, no team will be able to function properly. Ironically, taking the time to plot the course of action needed helps to free up time! It prevents leaders from being bogged down with *damage control* steps that may arise from unclear direction.

Another key element of timely delivery is review quality. Leaders should have regular reviews with their team to keep things on track. Reviews are a great way to ensure clarity, reward and give recognition to hard-working individuals, celebrate success, and stimulate improvement.

Leadership is a journey of growth. Staying on the path to success can be tricky. In the next chapter, we'll explore how leaders can manage and lead their teams successfully.

7

MANAGING AND LEADING SUCCESSFULLY

Hamza Khan made interesting observations in his *Stop Managing, Start Leading* TED Talks of 2016. In this talk, he shares the real reason why he decided to quit a past job. Hamza admits that he always showed up late for work. One morning, his manager decided enough was enough, an example had to be made. That fateful morning, Hamza showed up 15 minutes late for work. The manager concluded that it seemed like Hamza simply was not pulling his weight and that his tardiness was negatively impacting team morale. The Ted Talks speaker admits that this assumption was the straw that broke the camel's back.

As managers and leaders, we sometimes erroneously presume productive team members are chained to their desks. Rather than make a scene, Hamza decided to get some petty revenge instead. For the last two weeks on the job, he showed up early and spent the entire work day doing one thing only: watching movie marathons. Every day, Hamza would walk by the manager's desk, and without fail, the manager seemed satisfied. This baffled Hamza. He sat in the office and did nothing but watch movies all day, yet this seemed to make the manager happy. He vowed from that moment onward that he'd never be managed again. Hamza admits that managers have tried and failed, which left him to wrestle with a paradox: Organizations and teams need management, but people hate to be managed. This led him to explore the question if millennials should be managed.

Those who criticize millennials often point out that they are lazy, entitled, disloyal, unmotivated, and selfish. Research estimates that by 2025, millennials will make up 75% of the global workforce (Tina, 2021). This impressive figure highlights the need for transformation in management and leadership models, because Generation Y is built for tomorrow's workplace. Think about it. Millennials were raised in an increasingly connected and flat world, necessitating that they become increasingly resourceful, agile, and entrepreneurial. Modern managers and leaders need to realize that how and why millennials work is fundamentally out of sync with the expectations of tradition.

It is not uncommon for millennials to have a portfolio of work, specialize in numerous fields, change jobs frequently, and be connected to their work wherever the coffeehouse Wi-Fi is best.

Why is it then that so many millennials are still being managed like factory workers of old? The simple answer is tradition. If you trace the management history back far enough, you'll end up in the Industrial Revolution. The Industrial Revolution was a turning point. For the first time, we saw organizations achieve a much larger scale. Managers played a vital role in keeping a company's growth going. Another office relic, the eight-hour workday, can trace its roots to this time as well. The eight-hour work was proposed by a social reformer named Robert Owen. He suggested that our days should be divided into three equal parts for work, sleep, and play to achieve better work–life balance. By the mid-20th century, we started to develop theories on management.

From there, management continued to evolve, until the father of management thinking, Peter Drucker, noticed a paradigm shift. He noticed that the most valuable assets for future businesses will be knowledge workers and their productivity. Drucker first coined the phrase *knowledge worker* in 1959, well before the arrival of millennials. Based on the history of management and

Drucker's observations, it becomes painstakingly clear that what businesses need in the digital age is a fresh approach to management.

The old *command and conquer* mindset of traditional management models simply won't appeal to millennials because it does not make sense. It does not make sense for creative agencies, start-ups, think tanks, or anywhere the next generation is trying to apply their skills in creative, entrepreneurial, or information-based work. Yet many managers and leaders choose to embrace a traditional approach. Tradition may be comforting and easy, but it stifles innovation. One cannot move forward if one's gaze is firmly fixed in the past.

Doing things because of tradition is, frankly, an awful reason to continue doing so. It behooves the leaders and managers of the next generation to approach the topic with a new mindset. Traditional models of management rest on the assumption that workers are lazy and dislike to work. This way of thinking assumes that work is a chore and that workers will need supervision. It's comparable to doing the chores you hated as a child. Modern work demands of managers and leaders to assume the exact opposite, that employees are ambitious and self-motivated, and given the proper conditions, leadership can help these employees achieve personal and professional excellence.

What are the proper conditions? In my experience, I found that it starts from a place of trust. This is a trust that employees or team members show up for the right reason that they want to work. They have their responsibilities, goals, and deadlines. I give team members space, physical and otherwise. Nobody can deliver their best work when someone is breathing down their neck. As long as work gets done on time and it adheres to quality standards, there is no real need for employees to be chained to a desk. Encourage an environment of co-creation so that employees can become emotionally invested in the process of collaborating.

There is no denying that the difference between leadership and management exists, but it's not as clear-cut as one might assume. Roles simply dictate responsibilities. The true difference between the two lies in mindset, the conceptions they embrace deep in their psyches. Those who gravitate toward the manager's way of doing things tend to embrace process, like stability, and have a habit of wanting to resolve problems quickly—sometimes before a problem is fully understood. Those who embrace a leadership mindset tend to have a better tolerance for chaos and are willing to explore issues more fully (Zaleznik, 2004).

MANAGING EFFECTIVELY

There are certain skills without which you won't become an effective manager. These are critical skills that help us lead and encourage the team. Let's explore the skills needed to elevate one's managerial game to the next level.

Knowing What the Team Needs and Don't Need

Effective managers are in touch with their team. They know what their team needs to stay productive and work effectively. These managers strive to contribute to a harmonious workplace. Team members need to know that their efforts affect the bigger picture. These managers are mindful of the behaviors that can discourage success in their teams. As a manager, you are the most significant factor that will impact how motivated your team is. Managers play a central role in culture, performance management, job design, and reward systems—the things that impact team motivation.

Shockingly, 84% of American workers pointed out that poorly trained managers create unnecessary stress and work, a recent study found (SHRM, 2020). The study also found that more than half the respondents indicated that managers in their workplace could benefit from training. The top skills study participants felt managers could improve were communication, team building, time management, delegation, and creating an inclusive and positive team culture. It's an open secret that poor management is often cited as the reason why team members leave.

The biggest obstacle to management success is being a person who inspires others to follow. People have rational reasons and irrational motivations for their decisions. Every action you take will determine if you inspire loyalty in your team or not. Keep in mind that without that loyalty, management and leadership turn into a chore!

Nurturing Effective Interpersonal Relationships

Team members rely on a manager to treat them with dignity, respect, and attentiveness. Team members expect managers to display character and dependability under challenging circumstances. Managers who are open to receiving feedback from peers and reporting team members have made active listening and two-way feedback their communication standard. They understand and harness the power of interaction to encourage team members and peers to see the bigger picture.

Knowing the Financial Numbers of the Business

Successful managers understand the money side of the business and set goals accordingly, keeping track of team progress and success along the way. This helps the team to feel more connected to the goals that they are reaching and instills a sense of progress and purpose. Keep in mind that people want to know their performance measures up against expectations at work. Good managers understand this and play an active role in creating a supportive feedback loop for their teams.

Financial numbers can be a vague term, so let's clarify. Successful managers can highlight key elements of an income statement, discuss methods for forecasting costs and revenues, explain the importance of performance measurement, and introduce potential revenue streams. Looking at an organization's financial structure allows us to evaluate how funding was used and tracked over time. Some questions managers should consider when evaluating financial structures include the following:

- What is the cost to operate?
- What drives cost and revenue for the business?
- What are the revenue and payment streams for the business?
- How are investments financed?

Best practices for forecasting costs and revenues can be useful to evaluate the financials, and every manager and leader is encouraged to become familiar with them. These practices are

- ***Creating and using a revenue and cost manual***: Certain costs should be expected for your business regardless of size or performance. These are known as fixed costs. Then there are variable costs that are influenced by many factors. A revenue and cost manual will give you a better idea of these costs and can assist in creating accurate estimates. Keep in mind that the accuracy of estimates is dependent on how well market demand is anticipated for the product or service that your business provides.
- ***Using suitable estimation methods***: Four main methods can be used to predict revenue, expenses, and capital costs for an organization. Each method has different requirements for the level of math mastery and data that is needed. The straight line technique requires minimal math mastery but relies heavily on historical data to be accurate. This technique is used to display a constant growth rate. The moving average is used in repeated forecasts, makes use of historical data, and requires a minimal level

of math mastery. Complex methods like simple linear regression are used to compare one independent and dependent variable to each other but require statistical knowledge and the observation of a sample group to be of any use. A more advanced version of this method is called multiple linear regression, and it is used to compare multiple independent variables to one dependent variable.

- *Testing different assumptions*: As part of the projection process, alternative assumptions should be tested to understand the range of possibilities and sensitivity of results to key assumptions. Assumptions causing wider variation may warrant additional analysis and discussion among decision-makers. Consider best and worst-case scenarios.
- *Projecting multiple years*: Forecasts usually span three to five years. After the budget estimates have been made, the forecaster's job is not over. For the sake of accurate future forecasts, you'll need to monitor the accuracy and update the estimates.
- *Comparing real data against estimates*: Forecasts are both a science and an art. Uncertainty and variability cannot be eliminated. This is why we adopt best practices

where possible. Measuring performance keeps people accountable and can serve as a guiding light for improvement.

They Grasp What It Means to Be an Effective Manager

Biases are a part of human nature. We are fed with varying degrees of "us and them" mentalities since the day we are born, but the successful manager realizes that these biases can be harmful in a diverse workplace. They strive to keep their biases in check and take a page out of leadership's book instead: establishing a public modus operandi. If you want people to perform well, you need to enable them to do so. Similarly, if you want facts, then you need to establish an objective reputation and steer clear of playing favorites. Leading by example is a fantastic way to set the pace for expectations and behavior (Heathfield, 2020). When we are consistent in our speech and actions, others will notice, creating a foundation of trust in the process. It is important to communicate through our actions to our team members that we care about their careers and progress. When managers make the development of team members a priority, they are rewarded with high-functioning and harmonious teams.

LEADING EFFECTIVELY

All the free food and beanbags in the world could not stem the tide of the Great Resignation. We all have our reasons for changing jobs, but there is no question that the global pandemic completely changed the way we approach work. Many factors triggered the Great Resignation, including:

- employees reevaluating life priorities
- employers demanding a return to the office after remote work became a new normal
- mistreatment from employers and customers during the health crises that pushed employees to look for greener pastures
- some people who could not find suitable childcare services as schools embraced remote learning, while others did not comply with vaccination requirements

Notably, the top reasons given by workers in a recent survey were cited as low pay and lack of advancement opportunities (Fontinelle, 2022). Many factors contributed to the Great Resignation, but I firmly believe that leadership's misunderstanding of an entire generation had a lot to do with it.

As we discovered earlier, millennials make up the largest part of the global workforce. Those same millennials also tend to place more emphasis on work–life balance and well-being. As a result, millennials move more freely between jobs than previous generations. They are a confident, independent, and achievement-driven generation, who tends to be more socially and environmentally conscious than their predecessors. In addition, millennials are considered to be a tech-savvy generation, making them a hot commodity in the job market. So why is it that so many leaders complain that millennials are hard to manage?

We need to keep in mind that a broader context is at play here. Millennials are a generation impacted by many societal and technological trends. Parenting strategies changed, and social media and mobile devices have become the norm. These elements change how people live and work. When millennials entered the workforce, leaders had to face the challenge of accommodating and understanding a group of people with very different values and expectations from previous generations. As a result, Generation Y is often spoken about in the media, studied, and stereotyped. However, millennials are surprisingly quick to adapt to change, which is a valuable skill in today's fast-paced world.

There are many reasons why millennials willingly walk out of jobs, but burnout ranks among the top problems. Research by Deloitte found that 84% of millennials experienced burnout at their current jobs (Petit, 2022). With that much burnout going around, it is not surprising that more people are willing to quit their jobs. I look at that statistic from another angle: 84% of millennials experienced poor leadership at their current employment. My reason for this is simple. Burnout among employees is a symptom of poor management. Poor management, in turn, is a symptom of leadership that needs to evolve and mature. Effective leadership means

- *Consistency.* For leadership to be effective, you must be consistent. This means rewarding or discouraging the same behaviors when they appear and treating everyone in the same levelheaded way. Consistency also means being predictable and reliable in your actions as a leader. Consistency is the glue that holds multidisciplinary teams together, as they can trust their leader to behave fairly and deliver on promises made.
- *Crystal clear and thorough communication.* How we communicate with our teams will dictate our eventual success or failure. Whether you

are relaying instructions, sharing company updates, or recapping meetings, strive to keep your communications clear, thorough, and accurate. This goes for emails, face-to-face communications, phone calls, virtual meetings, and other forms of communication. Clear and accurate communication is vital to keep teams on the same page.
- *Making teamwork a goal.* The best teamwork happens when people work toward a goal. These goals should provide a unified focus and purpose to inspire the team to work together. Try to avoid setting goals for a single individual, as it isolates team members and can negatively impact performance.
- *Rewarding and recognizing excellence.* When team members do something exceptional, it is only right to reward them. This reward could be a vocal recognition, a bonus, or even a trophy. It is a good idea to present this reward in front of the team, as this will make the individual feel good and can inspire the rest of the team to work hard. Just remember to be consistent; otherwise, you'll run the risk of being seen as playing favorites.
- *Valuing the individual.* Leadership is a team sport, but we need to keep in mind that our

teams are made up of individuals who have unique strengths, weaknesses, and preferences. Trying to mold, motivate, and encourage these individuals with a one-size-fits-all approach is not effective. Instead, exceptional leaders customize their approach to fit the individual they are addressing for the best results.

TAKING A CLOSER LOOK AT ETHICS

Ethical leadership is a prerequisite for excellence. There are many reasons why I say this. When we lead by example, we do more than model good behavior. We provide the direction for ethical behavior. In turn, those around us observe this and act accordingly. More than that, being an ethical leader is essential to maintain credibility and a good reputation. Leadership is a long game, and behaving unethically will take leaders out of the A-League. As a result, their company or brand can be damaged. On a deeper level, unethical behavior corrodes self-esteem. In the long run, this can lead to many missed opportunities. Ethical leadership boils down to these main points:

- ***Honesty and justice***: Presenting the facts truthfully, being fair toward competitors, and communicating openly with others create trust

in those around us. Fairness rests on showing no favoritism, affording equal opportunities, and condemning harmful actions.
- **Respect and integrity**: Respect is earned and rightly so. People need to give respect to earn respect, regardless of position, characteristics, or other factors. These leaders value diverse thinking and foster inclusion. When we are consistent in our actions and values, we are displaying integrity to the people around us. We keep our word, follow through on decisions, and ensure that our actions are aligned with our values.
- **Responsibility and transparency**: As discussed in "Chapter 4: Leader Responsibility," responsibility is about embracing the power and duties that come with being in charge of something. It means being present in difficult situations and being responsive. Transparency is about open communication, acceptance of feedback, and disclosing information people would need to do their work. It is inextricably intertwined with responsibility.

Leaders play a vital role in the business world. What most interested me was the values that successful, ethical leaders had in common. Closer observations of many well-known ethical leaders revealed interesting insights. These leaders

- ***Know their internal compass***: By knowing yourself, your values, and your principles, it becomes easier to make them visible to others and confidently enter negotiations.
- ***Don't mind the repetition***: Leadership can't be rushed. It needs to be nurtured, and that takes time. Leaders are aware that their position also places them in a spot of vulnerability. Trust is built on the foundation of reputation, so if leaders misbehave, that trust can fade quickly.
- ***Stay true to ethical codes***: They don't bend the rules to help out a buddy if they act against the code of conduct that governs the organization or team. Turning a blind eye when someone acts against the code is not a good thing. It signals that the code is simply a footnote and, therefore, not important. To be guided by ethics means leaders cannot make exceptions and they clearly communicate which behaviors are not tolerated. By doing this, they build credibility, avoid confusion, and build consistency in their teams.
- ***Make their voices heard***: Overlooking important details can lead to significant damage. Ethical

leaders are aware of this and are willing to voice their concerns, even if what they have to say is unpopular. Even if it means slowing a project down or assigning more work, these leaders base their concerns and recommendations on their observations and potential problems spotted.
- *Admit mistakes*: When the pawpaw hits the fan, ethical leaders will not hide, minimize, or gloss over what happened. They know that if they do, they risk further repercussions. Instead, they own up to the mistake, issue an apology, and explore ways to remedy the situation. By facing these situations head-on, we communicate through our actions that we care and that we are doing everything we can to improve the situation. Actions speak louder than words after all.
- *Don't fear responsibility*: These leaders are willing to take full responsibility for unfavorable outcomes. They understand that as leaders, we can share in all the success, but we also need to take responsibility. There is a balance that needs to be maintained. We can't have one without the other.
- *Got their team's back*: These leaders can be counted on to show up for their teams and

speak for them when needed. They are present in the good times and bad. Most notably, these leaders occupy their roles in a selfless capacity, serving the interests of the group, team, or company above their own.

- *Act with fairness*: A leader's behavior should support meritocracy, ensuring the fair treatment of all parties involved. When we act with fairness, our actions communicate that we favor long-term wins and not short-term gains. This inspires trust and loyalty in followers.
- *Practice what they preach*: Ethical people hold themselves accountable to the same standards that they expect of others; otherwise, their credibility and reputation can suffer.

Just about any leader with a strong moral compass displays these values. These values can be applied to any leader, from Nelson Mandela to that guy in the office who is always trying to do the right thing. The value of ethical leadership should not be overlooked. It is the glue that holds multidisciplinary teams and creatives together, increasing the sense of belonging. When the company, leadership, and employee values are aligned, everyone gets to benefit from the positive atmosphere. In addition to this, ethical behavior helps to

- *Improve relationships with the target market*: Ethical leadership and culture can encourage customers and clients to continue doing business with a certain organization. That's good news for the company's bottom line and reputation.
- *Inspire loyalty and improve morale*: People follow people. They don't follow titles. This is why leaders need to place a strong emphasis on values and ethics to create a positive work environment. With a solid foundation, the stress and tensions of daily operation will become like wind blowing against a solid tree.
- *Create stability*: Companies with ethical leaders at the helm are less likely to run aground due to internal factors. Investors know and appreciate this, making them more likely to invest.

Ethics in Practice

Leaders are in a position of power, so ethical leadership needs to focus on how this power is leveraged to make decisions, which actions are engaged in, and how it will influence others. As leaders, we are responsible for influencing those around us to perform actions, behave in certain ways, and complete tasks. Effective leadership influences processes, amplifies empowerment, and can stimulate change in the attitudes and values of followers. This nurturing facet of leadership can promote a high level of integrity and character, providing a strong foundation on which beliefs, values, and decisions can be based. An exceptional leader knows that there is room for improvement. They keep a close eye on their moral compass and demonstrate their ethics through

- *Choices in business partners*: The people we choose to do business with, whether they be employees, suppliers, customers, or someone else, say a lot about what we stand for. Make a conscious effort to choose ethical people to conduct business with.
- *Stating what they stand for*: It is not enough to know what we stand for; we need to communicate those values clearly. By doing this, we can avoid misunderstandings, and it makes it easier to find the right people to partner with.
- *Setting the example*: Our values are reflected in our behaviors. When we are on a journey to become ethical leaders, regular introspection can help us spot mismatches between our values and behaviors. These mismatches should be addressed before it becomes problematic or habitual.

- *Never asking team members to act against agreed-upon rules*: Rules are necessary to govern teams, organizations, and society at large. Ethical leaders will never ask team members and colleagues to violate rules that have been set in place. This can happen surprisingly easily! If there is a rule that team members are only supposed to work eight hours in a work day, the leader should not ask them to stay late. Being an ethical leader is all about consistency and setting a good example.
- *Being honest about the data*: Sugarcoating and lying about the truth never did anyone any favors. On the contrary, it creates more problems and false expectations which can undo everything we've worked toward.
- *Celebrating the development of team members*: Confident, ethical leaders encourage their team members to develop into the best version of themselves. Those team members might leap for another opportunity, but bear in mind that the purpose of leadership is not to keep people captive by hindering their growth. The purpose of leadership is to nurture the character of people, developing them into strong professionals.

- *Refusing to be fooled by the calm before the storm*: In any leadership scenario, whether you are a teacher, team leader, or the president of a multinational corporation, you will face challenges. While you can never be fully prepared for every eventuality, successful leaders strive to be aware of and prepared for possible worst-case scenarios. It is best to identify these scenarios early so the ethical impacts and possible solutions can be thoroughly investigated.
- *Acknowledging others*: The Na'vi of Pandora (from the movie *Avatar*) said it best: "I see you." Seeing someone in this sense means acknowledging other's successes and not taking credit for their work. This fosters loyalty, boosts performance, and improves team morale—all vital ingredients in the recipe for leadership success.

These values can translate into real-world scenarios in many different ways. For example, manufacturing companies are expected to emphasize safety a lot. Meetings might start with a safety briefing, but this is not enough. Leaders need to demonstrate through their actions that safety is a priority. Simple actions such as using the handrail when climbing stairs, not using mobile phones in hazardous areas, and wearing safety gear when needed make a big difference.

Another area these values can shine is in marketing. When creating marketing materials, it is best to be honest about the products or services offered. Let's say, we've advertised a new cereal. It's a star-shaped, sugar-free, chocolate cereal. Now the customer who buys that box of cereal is expecting two things: First, if there is a representation of the product on the box, it should be accurate. Second, the cereal should be star-shaped, sugar-free, and chocolate-tasting. In other words, customers expect us to keep our promises. Delivering on those promises demonstrates consistency, creating bonds of trust with the target market.

In the office environment, these values can manifest in the preparation of sound contracts. The devil is in the details; this is why it is necessary to ensure that contracts have the necessary terms and conditions, payment terms, and scope of service detailed when working with external consultants, for example.

These values manifest on a personal level as well. The recommendations of people we deem ethical can carry more weight, as these people are viewed as credible. Ethical leaders will only recommend something if it has value, not because it will line their pockets. For example, a law firm might suggest to a client that an equal pay audit should be conducted to assess and mitigate risk. These suggestions provide value for the client, not the firm. Ethical leaders are aware of the weight that lies behind their recommendations; therefore, they will not make them lightly. Leadership ethics and the elements of successful leadership are two halves of the same whole. You need one to complete the other.

YOUR OPPORTUNITY TO MAKE A DIFFERENCE

Remember: Leaders show up to serve… and you can do that right now by helping your fellow leaders.

Simply by leaving your honest opinion of this book on Amazon, you'll point new readers in the direction of the leadership guidance they're looking for.

MAKE A LASTING IMPRESSION!

Thank you for your support. I wish you every success in your ventures. May you always succeed in being something more than average.

Scan the QR code below for a quick review!

CONCLUSION

Perhaps one of the most important insights I hope this book leaves the reader is this: Leaders show up to serve. They are not interested in providing for themselves only. They are interested in expressing themselves fully and developing those around them. These leaders know that proving oneself is a limiting concept. It applies a one-directional view that imposes boundaries and limits on the self. It is a viewpoint that is static and does not allow for periodic reinvention. Those interested in true leadership know that they need to be willing to take a hard look at themselves from time to time. They realize that leadership is a skill that needs to be nurtured, a road to be journeyed on. These individuals view life as an opportunity to bloom. It is about remembering what is important.

Leadership is a journey that engages with life. There is no set formula or rules to dictate any leadership style; it is a beautifully unique expression of your individuality. When people are arguing that they can't lead, they are usually thinking of managing people. There's a big difference, and while leadership and management are heavily blended, becoming a responsible, accountable leader involves

- a willingness to learn from past mistakes and insatiable curiosity
- developing your soft skills
- creating a compelling vision and then setting about to make that vision a reality
- developing a tolerance for uncertainty and a willingness to display a degree of daring
- personal development along the lines of improved self-knowledge, maturity, open-mindedness, welcoming criticism, and candor
- having self-confidence and staying true to yourself
- taking the time to reflect on answers, resolutions, and situations
- seeing and celebrating the small victories in daily life

Lastly, leadership involves not surrendering to the context of your life. Earlier approaches to leadership mainly focused on managing people, small matters, and achieving short-term results. When we embrace true leadership, we have two choices: to allow the context of our lives to permanently color our view of the world or treat it as the backdrop against which our particular brand of leadership will develop.

The path of a driven person is a relatively easy one, compared to the meandering walk leaders need to take at times. The driven person knows they need to get from point A to B, but the leader's path is not as clear-cut. It is consciously taken and filled with challenges that can lead to greater potential. As leaders, we need to declare independence against the age, culture, and estimation of others. Leaders occupy a strange space: They live in the world but exist outside existing conceptions thereof. That's because leaders create context. Leaders create new ways of doing things.

Another important theme in this book is leadership culture. Culture is created first and foremost by the leader and hinges on trust, honesty, and integrity. In turn, this encourages team members and colleagues to take ownership. Leaders who inspire a culture of trust are not afraid to be responsible and accountable for mistakes, nor are they leery of praising their team for successes. These leaders do what they can to create a positive, empowering environment for their team members to succeed. They do their best to steer clear of short-term thinking and the quick-fix mentality that seems to dominate workplaces everywhere. From my experience, the overreliance on quick fixes seems to stem from an addiction to convenience. Yes, those solutions may be quick, but there is no guarantee that they might not trigger more problems to develop. It also speaks of an unwillingness and lack of self-confidence in the leader who relies on these methods. They mistakenly believe they are doing the right thing and advancing their careers in the process. In truth, these leaders are tying themselves up with a rope of convenience. You see, the very thing that differentiates an exceptional leader from everyone else is their bravery and willingness to try new things while remaining accountable for the result.

Exceptional leaders embrace ownership. They believe in their ability to lead but are not driven by ego or personal gain. These people realize that leadership is a skill that needs to be nurtured with lots of small actions such as knowing team members' names, improving communication skills, and listening to different perspectives. True leadership is driven by a love for people, to see them succeed and excel in their roles. It is my sincerest hope that this book helped to shed some insight on different aspects of leadership. I'd love to know which leadership tip helped you the most, so feel free to leave me your impressions in the comments. On that note, I'll leave you with these parting words by Jim Rohn: "Leadership is the challenge to be something more than average."

BIBLIOGRAPHY

Agarwal, A. (2018, October 2). *Data reveals why the "soft" in "soft skills" is a major misnomer.* Forbes. https://www.forbes.com/sites/anantagarwal/2018/10/02/data-reveals-why-the-soft-in-soft-skills-is-a-major-misnomer/?sh=2a5b53846f7b

Barrow, C.-A. (2021, November 18). *Council Post: Five strategies for transitioning into a leadership role.* Forbes. https://www.forbes.com/sites/forbescoachescouncil/2021/11/18/five-strategies-for-transitioning-into-a-leadership-role/?sh=1f91dc111ff3

Bates, P. (2018, March 13). *5 practical approaches to overcoming your leadership fear.* About Leaders. https://aboutleaders.com/overcoming-leadership-fear/

Bertrams, A., Baumeister, R. F., & Englert, C. (2016). Higher self-control capacity predicts lower anxiety-impaired cognition during math examinations. *Frontiers in Psychology, 7.* https://doi.org/10.3389/fpsyg.2016.00485

Blome, C., Foerstl, K., & Schleper, M. C. (2017). Antecedents of green supplier championing and greenwashing: An empirical study on leadership and ethical incentives. *Journal of Cleaner Production, 152,* 339–350. https://doi.org/10.1016/j.jclepro.2017.03.052

Boxx, S. (2021, August 14). *Self-discipline: The prerequisite to leadership.* LinkedIn. https://www.linkedin.com/pulse/self-discipline-prerequisite-leadership-sarah-boxx-?trk=pulse-article_more-articles_related-content-card

Brennan, F. (2022, May 28). *How many trophies have Liverpool won? A complete list of all major silverware in the Reds trophy case.* The Sporting News. https://www.sportingnews.com/us/soccer/news/how-many-trophies-liverpool-won-list-silverware/slfx3wmamhgaqqd1t38uo4id

Brusman, M. (2021). *Managing with emotional intelligence: The power of empathy.* Working Resources. https://www.workingresources.com/

professionaleffectivenessarticles/managing-with-emotional-intelligence-the%20power-of-empathy.html

Building Champions. (n.d.). *8 elements of a successful leadership mindset.* https://www.buildingchampions.com/blog/8-elements-leadership-mindset

Bulgarella, C. (2018, September 21). *Purpose-driven companies evolve faster than others.* Forbes. https://www.forbes.com/sites/caterinabulgarella/2018/09/21/purpose-driven-companies-evolve-faster-than-others/?sh=28ec343c55bc

Calvello, M. (2022, April 6). *7 ways to take responsibility as a leader.* Fellow. https://fellow.app/blog/management/ways-to-take-responsibility-as-a-leader/

Capella University. (2018 March 12). *What employers mean by "good communication skills".* https://www.capella.edu/blogs/cublog/what-employers-mean-by-good-communication-skills/

Chiou, W.-B., Wu, W.-H., & Chang, M.-H. (2013). Think abstractly, smoke less: A brief construal-level intervention can promote self-control, leading to reduced cigarette consumption among current smokers. *Addiction, 108*(5), 985–992. https://doi.org/10.1111/add.12100

Collins, S. (2014, March 4). *Compassionate management: The softer side of leadership.* HRZone. https://www.hrzone.com/engage/managers/compassionate-management-the-softer-side-of-leadership

Conant, D. (2017, July 26). *Why taking responsibility is always the best leadership choice.* LinkedIn. https://www.linkedin.com/pulse/why-taking-responsibility-always-best-leadership-choice-conant

Cunningham, J. L., Sonday, L., & Ashford, S. (2022, September 5). *Are you afraid to identify as a leader?* Harvard Business Review. https://hbr.org/2022/09/are-you-afraid-to-identify-as-a-leader

Dickson, B. (n.d.). *Find your leadership purpose and write a leadership purpose statement.* Truist Leadership Institute. https://www.truistleadershipinstitute.com/publications-research/media-publications/find-your-leadership-purpose-and-write-a-leadership-purpose-statement

Duckworth, A. L., Peterson, C., Matthews, M. D., & Kelly, D. R. (2007).

Grit: Perseverance and passion for long-term goals. *Journal of Personality and Social Psychology*, 92(6), 1087–1101. https://doi.org/10.1037/0022-3514.92.6.1087

Edberg, H. (2022, January 20). 17 inspirational quotes on people skills. The Positivity Blog. https://www.positivityblog.com/17-inspirational-quotes-on-people-skills/

Eugene Therapy. (2020, June 11). *4 tips for building tolerance for others*. Eugene Therapy. https://eugenetherapy.com/article/4-tips-for-building-tolerance-for-others/

Fish, J. M. (2014, February 25). *Tolerance, acceptance, understanding*. Psychology Today. https://www.psychologytoday.com/us/blog/looking-in-the-cultural-mirror/201402/tolerance-acceptance-understanding

Fontinelle, A. (2022, May 5). *The Great Resignation*. Investopedia. https://www.investopedia.com/the-great-resignation-5199074

Forbes Human Resources Council. (2019, November 5). *12 dispute mediation techniques for managers*. Forbes. https://www.forbes.com/sites/forbeshumanresourcescouncil/2019/11/05/12-dispute-mediation-techniques-for-managers/?sh=3a7176563e86

Fuller, R., & Shikaloff, N. (2016, December 14). *What great managers do daily*. Harvard Business Review. https://hbr.org/2016/12/what-great-managers-do-daily

Gale, S. F. (2019, October 28). *Why diversity of thought is the key ingredient for better business*. American Express. https://www.americanexpress.com/en-us/business/trends-and-insights/articles/why-diversity-of-thought-is-the-key-ingredient-for-better-business/

Gleeson, B. (2021, April 8). *Leading with purpose: How to engage others with passion and focus*. Forbes. https://www.forbes.com/sites/brentgleeson/2021/04/08/leading-with-purpose-how-to-engage-others-with-passion-and-focus/?sh=3bac147222f1

Grover, S. (2017, November 30). *Do you have a controlling personality?* Psychology Today. https://www.psychologytoday.com/us/blog/when-kids-call-the-shots/201711/do-you-have-controlling-personality

Gulledge, C. (2018, July 27). *Nine steps to develop leadership discipline*.

Forbes. https://www.forbes.com/sites/forbescoachescouncil/2018/07/27/nine-steps-to-develop-leadership-discipline/?sh=3827c67a1fbe

Harrison, L. H. (2017, May 10). *New research reveals leadership accountability gap between performance and expectation.* PR Newswire. https://www.prnewswire.com/news-releases/new-research-reveals-leadership-accountability-gap-between-performance-and-expectation-300454356.html

Harter, J., Schmidt F., Agrawal, S., Plowman, S., & Blue, A. (2016, April). *The relationship between engagement at work and organizational outcomes.* Gallup. https://www.gallup.com/services/191558/q12-meta-analysis-ninth-edition-2016.aspx

Heathfield, S. M. (2020, June 6). *7 tips for effective management success.* LiveAbout. https://www.thebalancecareers.com/tips-for-effective-management-success-1916728

Heshmat, S. (2016, July 28). *How self-control can help you live a healthier life.* Psychology Today. https://www.psychologytoday.com/us/blog/science-choice/201607/how-self-control-can-help-you-live-healthier-life

Indeed Editorial Team. (2021a, February 23). *Your complete guide to building management experience.* Indeed. https://www.indeed.com/career-advice/resumes-cover-letters/management-experience

Indeed Editorial Team. (2021b, September 30). *The difference between responsibility vs accountability at work.* Indeed. https://uk.indeed.com/career-advice/career-development/responsibility-vs-accountability

Indeed Editorial Team. (2022, June 27). *Top 9 leadership skills to develop.* Indeed. https://uk.indeed.com/career-advice/career-development/leadership-skills

Jenkin, M. (2015, May 5). *Millennials want to work for employers committed to values and ethics.* The Guardian. https://www.theguardian.com/sustainable-business/2015/may/05/millennials-employment-employers-values-ethics-jobs

Jim Rohn quote. (n.d.). Quotefancy. https://quotefancy.com/quote/

67627/Jim-Rohn-Leadership-is-the-challenge-to-be-something-more-than-average

Kaufman, J. (2022, September 9). *Mindset matters: The strategy of time, disability, and the influence on the future of work*. Forbes. https://www.forbes.com/sites/jonathankaufman/2022/09/09/mindset-matters-the-strategy-of-time-disability-and-the-influence-on-the-future-of-work/?sh=4bf4e90b1dee

Kelfer, J. (2018, January 23). *Why genuine interest in others makes all the difference*. Jake Kelfer. https://www.jakekelfer.com/blog/why-genuine-interest-in-others-makes-all-the-difference

Llopis, G. (2013, June 3). *5 powerful ways leaders practice patience*. Forbes. https://www.forbes.com/sites/glennllopis/2013/06/03/5-powerful-ways-leaders-practice-patience/?sh=6f8f07bc421a

Martins, J. (2021, April 27). *How to lead by example: 4 tips from an Asana leader*. Asana. https://asana.com/resources/lead-by-example

Matusky, R. (2021, July 12). *How leaders demonstrate accountability*. ATD. https://www.td.org/user/content/randolphmatusky/how-leaders-demonstrate-accountability-02-15-20-08-38

Meyler, J. (2018, October 1). *Shifting your mindset – The four leadership attitudes to adopt right away*. GP Strategies. https://www.gpstrategies.com/blog/shifting-your-mindset-the-four-leadership-attitudes-to-adopt-right-away/

Nottingham Trent University. (2017, August). *Why is responsibility important in leadership?* https://online.ntu.ac.uk/online-student-experience/articles/what-is-responsible-leadership-and-why-is-important

Oppong, T. (2017, March 20). *Psychological secrets to hack your way to better life habits*. Observer. https://observer.com/2017/03/psychological-secrets-hack-better-life-habits-psychology-productivity/

Peters, S. (2013). *The chimp paradox: The mind management program to help you achieve success, confidence, and happiness*. TarcherPerigee.

Petit, M. (2022, May 2). *The Great Resignation: Why millennials are quitting their six-figure jobs*. Monitask. https://www.monitask.com/en/blog/the-great-resignation-why-millennials-are-quitting-their-six-figure-jobs

Prater, M. (2019, October 30). *Secrets of self-discipline: How to become supremely focused.* HubSpot. https://blog.hubspot.com/sales/self-discipline

Preterit, X. (2022, March 31). *Five reasons why leaders need a coach more than ever.* Forbes. https://www.forbes.com/sites/forbescoachescouncil/2022/03/31/five-reasons-why-leaders-need-a-coach-more-than-ever/?sh=20ebfcb677a5

Price, H. (n.d.). *Leadership accountability: Do you have it?* Jostle. https://blog.jostle.me/blog/leadership-accountability-do-you-have-it

Rais, S. (2022, September 9). *How to lose like a leader.* Forbes. https://www.forbes.com/sites/forbescoachescouncil/2022/09/09/how-to-lose-like-a-leader/?sh=4799620e3cf3

Rath, M. B. (2018, February 26). *Workforce productivity framework: How to address the needs of your entire workforce.* BDO Digital. https://www.bdodigital.com/insights/modern-workplace/workforce-productivity-framework

Routley, N. (2020, March 10). *How leadership accountability drives company performance.* Visual Capitalist. https://www.visualcapitalist.com/leadership-accountability-and-company-performance/

SHRM. (2020, August 12). *Survey: 84 percent of U.S. workers blame bad managers for creating unnecessary stress.* https://www.shrm.org/about-shrm/press-room/press-releases/pages/survey-84-percent-of-us-workers-blame-bad-managers-for-creating-unnecessary-stress-.aspx

Sluss, D. (2020, September 2). *Becoming a more patient leader.* Harvard Business Review. https://hbr.org/2020/09/becoming-a-more-patient-leader

Tina. (2021, May 29). *Millennials in the workplace statistics 2022: Latest trends.* TeamStage. https://teamstage.io/millennials-in-the-workplace-statistics/

Torch. (2021, March 10). *How accountability leads to successful management.* https://torch.io/blog/how-accountability-leads-to-success/

University of Illinois College of Agricultural, Consumer and Environmental Sciences (ACES). (2014, October 6). *Are leaders born or made?*

New study shows how leadership develops. ScienceDaily. www.sciencedaily.com/releases/2014/10/141006133228.htm

Vakil, T. (2019, November 28). *Lessons for leaders: Henry Ford failure story & bad leadership.* New Age Leadership. https://newageleadership.com/lessons-for-leaders-henry-ford-his-failure-story-bad-leadership/

VXI Marketing. (2021, December 2). *Taking ownership: A leader's best quality.* VXI. https://vxi.com/taking-ownership-a-leaders-best-quality/

Wiles, J., & Turner, J. (2022, April 29). *3 ways to build a sense of belonging in the workplace.* Gartner. https://www.gartner.com/smarterwithgartner/build-a-sense-of-belonging-in-the-workplace

Zak, P. (2017, January). *The Neuroscience of trust.* Harvard Business Review. https://hbr.org/2017/01/the-neuroscience-of-trust

Zaleznik, A. (2004, January). *Managers and leaders: Are they different?* Harvard Business Review. https://hbr.org/2004/01/managers-and-leaders-are-they-different

Printed in Great Britain
by Amazon